THE QUILTER'S GUIDE

TO PICTORIAL QUILTS

THE QUILTER'S GUIDE

GUIDE

TO PICTORIAL QUILTS

Maggi McCormick Gordon

COLLINS & BROWN

First published in Great Britain in 2000 by
Collins & Brown Limited
London House
Great Eastern Wharf
Parkgate Road
London SW11 4NQ

Editorial Director: Sarah Hoggett
Editor: Katie Hardwicke
Designer: Liz Brown
Jacket Designer: Fiona Knowles
Photographer: Matthew Ward

Front cover: *Beach Huts by Night* Lucy Hines
Back cover, from left to right:
Navajo Country Pamela Foxall
Greetings from Gafsa Margaret Ramsay
Going Places Jane E. Petty

1 3 5 7 9 8 6 4 2

British Library Cataloguing-in-Publication Data:
A catalogue record for this title is available
from the British Library.

ISBN 1-85585-769-3 (hardback)
ISBN 1-85585-846-0 (paperback)

Reproduced by Media Print Services
(UK) Limited
Printed by Dai Nippon, Hong Kong

Contents

introduction

THE ORIGINS OF pictorial quilts can be traced back to the early nineteenth century. Ever since, quilters have been discovering an infinite variety of ways to express their art. This chapter looks at the history of pictorial quilts and their development toward the pieces of textile art that are produced today.

Royal Clothograph (above and detail, left)
John Munro

The History of Pictorial Quilts

Within the long history of quiltmaking, pictorial quilts are the younger generation, developing from the simple appliqué motifs of the mid-nineteenth century to the complex pieces of textile art made today.

Most early quilts, used as bedcovers for warmth, were made either from one or several large pieces of fabric or small pieces, even scraps, stitched together at random or in patterns, with a layer of padding and finished with a backing. The layers were stitched together with running stitches that became known as quilting and were arranged into patterns. Sometimes motifs that created recognizable images were worked.

Folk-art themes frequently depict natural forms such as plants and animals, and many charming quilts from the mid-nineteenth century feature naive, folksy motifs. A good number of these designs, especially some of the flower and leaf motifs, were adapted into appliqué patterns.

When printed fabrics, especially cotton chintz from India, became popular in Europe in the eighteenth century, seamstresses often cut motifs from them and applied the pieces to plain backgrounds to make these expensive materials go farther. Some of these "broderie perse" quilts have the chintz pieces widely spaced, and the background is heavily quilted, often with trapunto added. Other examples show the

◀ **Cartoon coverlet** Martha Vail (Mrs. Peter Porter) Wiggins, mid-1800s

This unpadded bedcover, made in Saratoga, New York, illustrates humorous scenes of a type that were popular during the mid-nineteenth century. The figures – both people and animals – are drawn to scale and clothed in beautifully worked fabrics that give a comic realism to the sketches.

▶ **Mrs. Waterbury's Album Quilt** New Jersey, 1853

The inscription in the center block tells us that this well-designed album quilt was presented on "the 1st of April 1853 to the Rev. Mrs. Waterbury." We do not know what the occasion was, but many of the individual blocks are signed, some by men, some by women, and a few by groups of people. The motifs include religious images – several Bibles, a cross, the Wise Men – and patriotic ones, as well as flora, fauna, and geometric patterns.

cutouts arranged as a central medallion around which several borders have been added. Although many of the more realistic designs were organized on the background to create pleasing arrangements that became more pictorial as time went on, picture quilts did not really come into their own until the middle of the nineteenth century.

ALBUM QUILTS

Among the most beautiful of the early picture quilts were "album" quilts made as friendship or "freedom" quilts, and given to friends or relatives who were moving away to distant places, especially to the plains of the American Midwest.

Also known as presentation quilts or autograph quilts, they often depicted scenes of local interest, such as buildings or churches, and sometimes recognizable people or historical characters. Stylized flowers, leaves, and other forms from nature feature heavily, and some designs depict familiar objects, animals, and pets, as well as people going about their daily lives.

In some cases, different people made each block; in others, all the stitching was done by one or two quilters. The most famous album quilts were made in and around Baltimore, Maryland, between about 1840 and 1860. They are usually instantly recognizable for their white or cream backgrounds; heavy use of red, green, and yellow fabrics; and highly pictorial motifs arranged in blocks. They are almost all highly

▶ **Reconciliation Quilt**
Lucinda Ward Houstain, 1865

The blocks in this exquisite album quilt, its colors undiminished after more than 100 years, show episodes from the period immediately following the Civil War together with amusing depictions of exotic animals. Made by Lucinda Ward Houstain in Brooklyn, New York, it is, without a doubt, one of the most extraordinary quilts ever found.

▶ **Street scene**
Is the man on his horse a gentleman farmer come to town? Or is the entire panel a depiction of his Northern farm, with its animals and its proudly flown American flag?

▶ **The Liberty pavilion**
The patriotic pavilion, topped with flags and an eagle, and with Lady Liberty inside, is probably a representation of the "new" dome of the Capitol building in Washington, DC, which had been rebuilt and dedicated in 1863.

▶ **Free man or slave?**
The farm worker balancing a bucket and a basket is likely to be a freed slave working his own land. Perhaps he has come to town to sell his fresh milk and eggs.

complex, with intricate designs and often superb workmanship.

STORY AND SCENIC QUILTS

By the middle of the 1800s, a few quiltmakers were creating works based on biblical themes, particularly those with a religious or moral tale to tell. A number of bible story quilts made by African-American quilters, for whom the bible was a part of daily life, survive. They, along with examples that detail secular and even everyday life, have become known as "story" quilts.

In the early nineteenth century, quilts were sometimes made featuring realistic representations of ships, plants, and animals, and patriotic images like eagles, but traditional geometric patchwork patterns were far more common.

Quilts that attempt to create pictures – landscapes, for example – are relatively new and probably date from the early 1920s. Such pieces are by their very nature highly personalized representations, and it is difficult to generalize about them, except to say that each

▼ **Cotton Gin and Farm**
*c.*1895

Texture and naivety enliven this unsigned landscape from Pennyslvania. The mill, houses, and barns are silk and cotton appliqué, and many of the people, animals, and floral motifs are embroidered in bright silk thread. Some of the appliquéd animals are padded, giving them a rounded, realistic look.

▲ **Garden of Eden** Abby F. Bell Ross, c. 1874

This depiction of Adam and Eve under the Tree of Knowledge probably
had its roots in traditional Tree of Life designs. The beasts surrounding
Man and Woman are appliquéd and embellished with embroidered
details, while many of the flowers, insects, and animals are embroidered
in bright, mainly realistic colors. The narrow curved brown border
encloses the garden and its inhabitants while separating, but not
excluding, the water creatures at the bottom of the quilt.

piece is truly unique. Many of the surviving examples are made using a combination of patchwork and appliqué, worked from strips or small squares that give the piece a mosaic effect.

By the end of the twentieth century, the scenic quilt had become a standard part of the quilting repertoire, with landscapes vying for attention with portraits and realistic interpretations of natural forms. This book is a personal selection of some of the most interesting examples of the art of the contemporary pictorial quiltmaker.

▲ Reservation Quilt *c.* 1900

A stunning piece of appliqué, this unique quilt was made by members of the Sioux nation on the Crow Creek Reservation in South Dakota. Scenes of daily life are worked in red, yellow, blue, beige, and white with lightly embroidered details.

▶ John L. Sullivan *c.* 1888

The world heavyweight bare-knuckle boxing champion is celebrated on this heavily decorated silk and velvet crazy quilt, thought to have been made in Chicago because of the numerous references to the city embroidered in the patches.

designing pictorial quilts

DESIGNING A QUILT with a pictorial element is different from planning a geometric piece. Color and fabric play an equally important role, but creating a representational pictorial image using fabric and embellishment is a very different exercise from organizing traditional blocks.

Beach Huts by Night (detail)
Lucy Hines

Source Material

Pictorial quilts can derive from myriad sources. Many of the well-known makers of pictorial quilts are textile artists; they are trained in design and use fabric as their medium. But many of the quilts featured in the following pages are made by quilters who, without training in art and design, wanted to express an idea or feeling pictorially and by trial and error and experimentation have found an outlet for their creativity.

We all have an innate creative instinct, but sometimes it is hard for us to unlock the self-confidence to set about a completely original piece of work. Looking around for inspiration often provides the key we need to open a door to our creativity. Sources for pictorial work are everywhere. A good place to start is with photographs or drawings, your own or those found in books or magazines, postcards, designs on giftwrap or greeting cards. Perhaps you want to create a memento of a wonderful trip. Looking through your snapshots and the travel brochures and postcards you acquired along the way will probably spark off several thoughts. Making a piece that commemorates an important event – a birth, a wedding, an anniversary – in your family or for a friend can also start with a look through the family photo album.

▲ **Printed material**
Books, postcards and greeting cards, and magazines are all good sources for pictorial inspiration. You can use a reproduction of a photograph or drawing, or base your design on a picture of a colorful tile or mosaic.

▶ **Photographs and sketches**
Most of us carry a camera with us when we travel. If you get in the habit of snapping images that appeal to you – in shape or color, for example – you will soon build up a collection of source material that is personal to you. Having a small sketchbook at hand – we can *all* make rough sketches – will also pay dividends.

▼ Would Van Gogh Have Been a Quilter?

Wendy Lawson

PATCHWORK, APPLIQUE, HAND QUILTING

Using the natural world as a source of inspiration can lead in many different directions. This quilter has kept the design of this wall hanging simple, but the piecing, quilting, and choice of color are all more complicated than they might appear at first glance. The title of the piece occurred to her unexpectedly as she constructed it.

▲ Sunflower sources

Wendy Lawson is a dedicated gardener as well as a passionate quilter who finds inspiration in her own garden. For those who do not have a sunflower growing nearby, however, there are large numbers of representations on greeting cards, postcards, and famous works of art that might provide ideas and help in making decisions about color, shape, and positioning.

The beautifully shaded flower petals were cut with a rotary cutter using incremental progressions to make circles.

The dark triangles set into the pieced inner borders point the eye into the center of the piece.

Adapting Source Material

Finding source material to provide you with ideas and inspiration is only the beginning when you are designing a pictorial quilt. You will seldom find a single image that is the right size, the right color, and in the right position and combination to be used just as it appears. Even if you are portraying one individual item on your quilt – a flower or house or butterfly, perhaps – you will probably need a number of different images, some in several sizes, that represent the thing you want to depict. If you are assembling a more complex image, you may need various representations of the different elements you wish to include in the final picture.

RESIZING IMAGES

Most of us believe firmly that we "cannot draw," but when we are brave enough to try it, we often discover that we can make a recognizable sketch that is adequate for use as a design source. Laying out a few images that you want to include in a piece of work and sketching their basic shapes in various sizes will often give you a clearer plan that you can use as you work toward a final arrangement.

Once you have an idea of the overall design and its various aspects, you will almost certainly need to resize some of the different elements. Most modern photocopiers are equipped to enlarge and reduce images, making the task of sizing up or down much easier, and many of us take advantage of this facility from time to time. It is also possible to reduce and enlarge shapes on a drafting machine called a pantograph, for those who have access, and the box below shows a tried-and-tested method of carrying out the task by hand.

TRACING AND SIZING UP

Tracing a design and then adapting it to a different size is a relatively straightforward procedure. The only tools you need are a ruler and a pencil. You can use prelined graph paper, and tracing paper with a preprinted grid can be purchased, but neither is strictly necessary. The larger the grid, the larger your finished design.

1 Place a sheet of tracing paper over the image to be traced. Secure the paper with masking tape if necessary.

2 Draw a grid of horizontal and vertical lines, working to a specific size – here, we have used ½ inch (13 mm) – over the entire image to be resized.

3 On a separate sheet of paper, make a grid of the desired size. We have used 1-inch (25-mm) squares, which will double the size of the image. Draw the new image so each square corresponds to that in the original tracing.

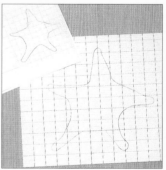

4 The shape has been enlarged quickly and easily to twice its original size. If the enlarged grid had been 2 inches (50 mm), the image would have been four times larger.

▲ Solomon and the Shulammite Diana Brockway
MACHINE APPLIQUE

Pictorial quilts can be adaptations of full-blown ideas. This
sumptuous piece, based on a wood engraving by the maker's son,
was adapted by enlarging and modifying some of the elements to
suit the use of fabric as its medium. The image was divided into
three parts – the right-hand side including most of Solomon, the
left-hand side including most of the Shulammite, and the middle
area including the crossed arms – and each was completed before
they were all joined together.

▶ Source material
The original woodcut was used as an
illustration for the Song of Solomon in
a modern bible. The details have been
transferred meticulously from hard wood
to soft textile.

Composition

Sometimes, when designing a new quilt, you have too many ideas. Scenes abound in your head, and you want to include several of them but still maintain coherence. Composition is the key to creating an impact that tells the story and focuses the viewer's attention where you wish.

Once you have chosen a theme, you will need to select a format (see box opposite). There are several ways of drawing the viewer into a picture and organizing the various elements into a coherent composition. Lead-in lines, such as a road or the sweep of a hill, draw the eye. Textural detail and hot colors in the foreground give a sense of depth. Placing the pictorial elements on a grid of thirds can also help to achieve a satisfying composition. This method, known as the rule of thirds, is a recognized artistic principle.

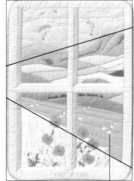

◄ **East Sussex** Heather Downie
PERSPECTIVE, DIAGONALS
Portrait format is used for this landscape of the English countryside, viewed through a window frame. The importance of diagonal lines in a composition is shown clearly, with the changes of color and tone in the fields highlighted by diagonal lines of quilting and the embroidered outlines in the hills beyond.

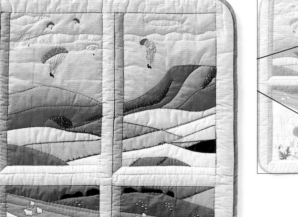

The white sheep, appliquéd and embroidered in the green pastures, emphasize the diagonal composition.

The bright red poppies in the foreground add color and texture that give a sense of depth.

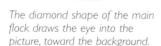

The straight horizontal line dividing the foreground from the middle ground is softened by the placement of the birds' bodies.

The diamond shape of the main flock draws the eye into the picture, toward the background.

▶ **Cape Gannets** June Worman
DIAGONALS, RULE OF THIRDS
The rule of thirds has been beautifully applied in the composition of this wall hanging, with large, clearly delineated birds in the foreground, sea and sky in the background, and a dense flock on the midground beach.

Zigzag quilting in the foreground adds visual tension to the area.

► **Groucho** Margaret Standish
DIAGONALS

Here, diagonal lines enhance the perspective, and the empty spaces around the screen offer a visual contrast to the striking impact of the figure and to the humor in the details found in the audience. Remember that to be successful, a composition always needs some empty space to direct the eye around the focal point at the center of interest of the picture.

The stitched diagonal lines lead the eye to the central, immediately recognizable figure of Groucho Marx.

The seating area fills the lower third of the picture, drawing the eye to the screen which fills the top two-thirds.

SELECTING A FORMAT

Pictures can have several shapes. Quilts are frequently square to fit a bed, and this format works especially well for geometric patterns. Wall hangings can be made in any shape, so consider different formats before making a final decision. A square format creates a stable, self-contained image that draws the eye into the middle of the composition. The portrait format is an upright rectangle that leads the eye vertically up and down, and is ideal for tall subjects. The landscape format, in which the eye is taken from side to side, is widely used, not surprisingly, for landscape compositions. When selecting a format, think about the balance of foreground and background, and the position of the horizon or focal point.

▲ **Cropping a photograph with Ls**
Looking at a photograph or drawing using a homemade viewfinder can help you decide on the best format. Simply cut two L-shaped pieces of cardboard and place them over the picture. See how the image looks if it is square as opposed to vertical or horizontal, for example, or what happens visually if some of the empty space is eliminated.

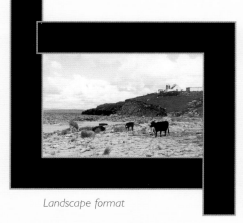

Landscape format

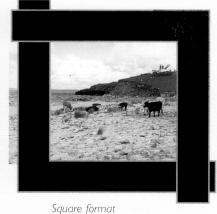

Square format

Portrait format

Using Perspective

Perspective is a term that describes the depiction of spatial relationships on a flat surface – creating a three-dimensional image on a flat two-dimensional surface. The rules of perspective apply to landscapes where the horizon is an obvious line, as well as to figures and interior spaces where the horizon is unseen but implied.

The principles of linear perspective are most clearly found in landscapes and can be applied by making sure that parallel lines, such as roads or rivers, appear to converge toward a "vanishing point" on the horizon. Lines above the horizon slant down and those below slant up, as shown in the quilt of Venice, below. Objects, such as trees or houses, also appear to become smaller as they recede into the distance and their shapes distort.

Aerial perspective, where colors become cooler toward the horizon, is another principle that can be exploited by the pictorial quilter to good effect. Depth and distance can be successfully conveyed by contrasts of tone and texture, with warmer colors (reds and oranges) in the foreground and cool shades (blues and greens) toward the horizon. A textured foreground enhances this contrast. Think about the relative size of objects; overlapping them is a simple way to add recession.

But for the complementary color of her dress, the figure glimpsed through the gateway would be almost lost.

The lines of the rooftops and the edges of the canal converge as they head toward the vanishing point, beyond the arch.

◀ Venetian Adventure
Jackie Evans and Betty Standiferd
LINEAR PERSPECTIVE, VANISHING POINT

Perspective has been beautifully realized in this cityscape of an immediately recognizable Venice. Beyond the bridge, the canal turns, and the angle from which we see the houses changes, too, while the boats moored along each bank decrease in size as they disappear under the bridge's arch. The reflections are masterful.

Reflections must also obey perspective, both in terms of their position and their scale.

▲ Off-center
The vanishing point does not have to be in the center of the picture, nor does it need to be visible in the composition, as long as you know where it lies and organize the design to take account of it.

The color of the trees and the landforms varies from light to dark to create visual texture and a strong aerial perspective.

The water that appears under the bridge and behind it is shaded to add to the sense of distance.

◀ Beyond the Dragon Gate Kate Molloy
AERIAL PERSPECTIVE

The river is conveyed in the right-hand bottom quadrant of this wall hanging as two lines decreasing in width, but not converging. The perspective is achieved more through the shading of the riverbanks and the foliage, and the contrasts of visual texture afforded by the use of strips of triangular pieces, than by using the technique of linear perspective.

The tones of the fabric used for the trees become softer as they recede into the distance.

The use of fretwork in the foreground adds texture that enhances the feeling of depth.

▲ Focal point
The focus of the image is the simple, elegant Chinese bridge over the river, which is well in front of any vanishing point that might be found on the line of the horizon.

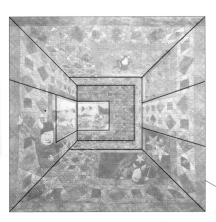

The desert scene retains its own perspective when the background turns the corner.

Designed to have an impact when seen from a distance, the quilt also has little surprises like the animals hiding in the desert sand.

◀ Because the Cyclist Loves His Mum
Marie Roper
3D PERSPECTIVE

Playing with perspective is a tricky business, but this quilt, based on the works of Dutch artist M.C. Escher, a particular favorite of the quilter and her son for whom it was made, successfully uses a "complex series of arrangements … to tell three stories: time passing, different perspectives, and the cyclist's journey" across the western deserts of the United States.

◀ Three dimensions
Are we looking into a cube from the top? At the far wall of a room? The corners converge and the geometric forms get smaller as they near the central square.

The lines of machine quilting meet at the corners and change direction to reinforce the 3D effect.

Choosing Colors

Color is perhaps the most exciting aspect of quiltmaking, and its role in the success and impact of a pictorial quilt is critical. There is an infinite variety of colored fabrics available from which the quilter can choose, so a basic understanding of color theory will help you make a successful selection.

COLOR BASICS

Color theory is based on a color wheel that shows the relationship of the basic colors. There are three primary colors: red, yellow, and blue. These three can be combined (on a painter's palette) to make all the other colors of the rainbow, although black and white are needed to achieve a degree of shading.

Combining any two primaries will yield another color – a secondary – and mixing a primary with a secondary will yield a tertiary, or intermediate, color.

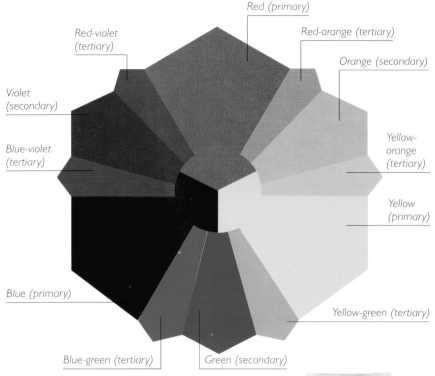

Red (primary)
Red-orange (tertiary)
Red-violet (tertiary)
Orange (secondary)
Violet (secondary)
Blue-violet (tertiary)
Yellow-orange (tertiary)
Yellow (primary)
Blue (primary)
Yellow-green (tertiary)
Blue-green (tertiary)
Green (secondary)

▲ Color wheel
A color wheel is a circular device used by designers and artists to show the relationship between the primary, secondary, and tertiary colors.

Yellow and violet

▶ Complementary colors
Colors that appear opposite one another on the color wheel – usually a primary and a secondary – are called complementary and can be combined to provide visual contrast and tension, and give a lively feel to a pictorial quilt.

Blue and orange

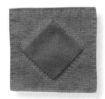

Red and green

◀ Lilies Sheila Acton
COMPLEMENTARY COLORS, ANALOGOUS COLORS, SHADING

Blue and orange are complementary colors used to great advantage on this beautifully shaded piece inspired by the wild lilies on the island of Madeira. The masterful use of white, combined with analogous color for the pink petals and green leaves of the flowers, complements the hand-dyed background, which is itself shaded on a much larger scale.

You can use the color wheel to help you to select colors. Complementary colors are pairs that appear opposite each other on the wheel. When they are placed alongside each other, both colors look stronger. Complementaries can be used to make a figure or motif stand out from its surroundings.

Analogous colors lie next to each other on the color wheel. A selection of three such colors, perhaps blue, blue-green, and green, would make a harmonious color scheme.

When the same color is used in a myriad of different shades, tints, and patterns to make a color scheme that ranges from light to dark, it is called monochromatic. Combining two highly contrasted monochromatic color schemes can create a visual richness.

White used with a bright or dark color will make the color leap from the background, while using black will make bright or pale colors glow.

COLOR VALUE AND CONTRAST

The lightness or darkness – the shade or tint – of a color is called its value, and is often more important in conveying the desired impression than the color itself. It is easy to sort very light colors from dark ones, but there will invariably be a large group of middle tones. These receive their perceived value from the color of the fabric next to them. If a stark contrast is required, fabrics with very different values will need to be juxtaposed. If a blending is required, the values must move gently from dark to light.

BLENDING AND SHADING

The contrast required to make successful pictorial images in fabric is often very subtle, and the choice of color, and to some extent pattern, becomes critical when a blending from light to dark needs to be achieved smoothly but in a small space. You can either use analogous colors or a selection of shades of one color.

detail from **Mature-i-tree** Iris Taylor

detail from **Face the Future – Millennium Dawn** Liz Hands

▲ Harmonious colors
Here, the color of fall leaves – reds, oranges, and yellows with a touch of brown – is based on a selection of analogous colors that provide harmony to great effect.

▲ Blending colors
Blending the tones from the dark strands of hair behind the hairband to the highlight on the nose, with the pale cheek between, has been achieved through the selection of a number of fabrics based on a single color.

Choosing Fabrics

Selecting fabrics for pictorial quilts presents the opportunity to experiment with unusual weaves. Fragile materials such as silk and satin, or heavy-duty upholstery cloth that is too stiff to use in a geometric quilt, can all be employed to great effect along with loosely woven utility fabrics and those with a distinct nap or pile.

Texture can be created visually by juxtaposing colors and prints and plains, or by using textured fabrics such as slub silk or devore velvet.

There is a vast selection of printed fabrics that can be used very effectively to convey an idea or image. Some quilters prefer to hand color their own fabrics, either by painting or dyeing.

Curling waves have been machine-quilted on the pieced circle.

The central seagulls were made by machine and quilted before being applied for a 3D effect.

◀ **Before the Storm**
Barbara Middlebrook

HAND PAINTING

The entire background of this variation of the traditional Storm at Sea patchwork block was hand painted to create the sky, sea, horizon, breakers, and sandy shore. The paper-pieced circle is made from beautifully contrasted shades of brown, tan, and beige and inset into the background.

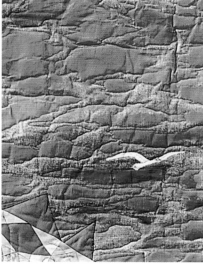

▲ **Painted sky**

A few high-flying gulls have been applied to the hand-painted sky background, free-machine quilted to give the effect of clouds.

◀ **Beechwood** Deirdre Rodwell
TEXTURED FABRICS
Strips of blue and green fabric are
staggered and joined to evoke an
impressionistic but completely
recognizable bluebell wood underneath
tree tunks made from a selection of
textured silk. The sky was hand dyed.
Many commercial fabrics that emulate
the visual texture of hand dyeing are
available in a good choice of colors.

*Turning the fabric so that
the lines of texture run in
different directions adds to
the realism.*

USING PRINTED FABRICS

The careful selection of printed fabrics to use in a
pictorial quilt can lift a piece of work from the mundane
to a higher level of design success. Color, value, and
texture, both visual and actual, are important
considerations, along with the scale of the printed
pattern. Be careful that the design on the fabric does not
overwhelm the patterns around it, and make sure the
shades of color blend the way you want them to.

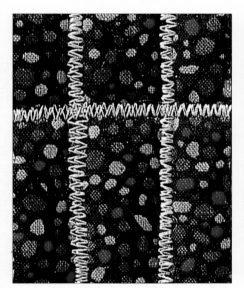

detail from **The Barn Church** Deborah Fife

▲ **Stained glass**
This fabric sat in the maker's stash for many
months before it took its well-chosen place
as the stained glass windows of a local
landmark church in her neighborhood.

detail from **How Does Your Garden Grow?
It Doesn't!** Margaret Syrett

▲ **Reversed fabric**
Turning the fabric from front to back
creates a clever shaded effect to represent
the underside of the leaves of a dying plant,
which even the ladybugs are unable to save.

detail from **Where Land Meets Water**
Inge Mardal and Steen Hougs

▲ **Small prints**
Small-patterned fabrics are used to create
the water, sandbar, and stones along the
shoreline. Small-scale prints blend better for
pictorial work than larger patterns.

Creating Texture with Quilting

Surface texture adds vitality to any quilt. Most scenic quilts work best if they convey a feeling of depth, and this can be reinforced by the quilting: follow the rules of perspective (see page 24) and stitch lines in the background closer together than those in the foreground of the scene.

Abstract designs also need textural contrasts. Meander (or stipple) quilting, for example, gives a dense, close-textured feel; outlining shapes with a line or two of simple quilting will call attention to that area of the work, while a simple cross-hatched grid will diminish its overall impact.

► **Wedding Fan** Gill Tanner
HAND QUILTING

The simple shape of this highly effective piece is reinforced by its quilted and beaded struts. The outlined ribbon and hearts retain a three-dimensional feel.

▲ **Beach Huts by Night** Lucy Hines
HAND QUILTING

Straight lines of quilting depict the straight wooden planks and some of the roofs of the huts, while the rounded pebbles on the beach are conveyed by means of meander quilting. The moon's rays radiate to the left and stop against the curves of the quilted waves.

► **Walk Like an Egyptian** Jacky Raeburn
MACHINE QUILTING

Quilting has been worked only on the background areas, causing the sunburst appliqué patches and the figure to stand out. The increasing density of the stitching from the foreground to the background of the landscape creates a strong sense of distance and perspective.

The widely spaced quilting reinforces
the feeling of the vastness of the
desert landscape.

The figure is on a separate
piece of fabric appliquéd to
the background.

Embellishments

Perhaps the best part of making a pictorial quilt is decorating the finished piece. Any form of embellishment can be used, provided it enhances the design and adds a bit of pizazz without becoming overpowering.

Textured quilting methods, such as cording and stuffing (trapunto), are widely used, as is surface embroidery. French knots, laid work, and all manner of standard hand embroidery stitches can be employed with great effect, and although machine embroidery generally becomes part of the construction process, it can also be used to highlight areas effectively.

Beads, buttons, and sequins come in an astonishing array of colors, sizes, and types and add sparkle in a unique way, while shells and other found objects – leaves, flowers, bits of string or rope, pieces of wood – can all contribute to a successful composition.

Three-dimensional creations, such as insects on flowers or tassels on fans, can be made to your own design and applied to the surface, and readymade appliqué motifs or cutouts from patterned fabric can be used in similar ways. Ribbons, lace, yarn, nets, and decorative embroidery thread can all be employed effectively.

▶ **Clockwork** Anja Townrow
EMBELLISHED WITH WATCH AND CLOCK FACES
This wall hanging, made to commemorate the millennium celebrations, is based on a pocket watch inherited from the maker's uncle. The interlocked wheels are decorated with buttons and watch faces – "anything round."

DECORATIVE DETAILS

Good design is frequently found in the details. Pictorial quilts can be greatly enhanced by the careful addition of extras, embellishments that tie in with the theme of the quilt or various techniques used in creating it. Remember, though, that less can be more, and avoid overworking a piece with too much decoration.

detail from **Glory of the Deep** Hava Salter

detail from **Sail Away** Sarah Hadfield

detail from **Shinto Sunrise** Jenni Dobson

detail from **Cissa Ceastre – Chichester** Patricia McLaughlin

▲ **Manipulated fabric**
Yo-yos, or Suffolk puffs, make excellent clusters of 3D images. Ruching and gathering, folding and pleating can all add texture and interest.

▲ **String and cord**
This nautical knot is tied from rope. Various weights of thread and yarn can be tied in knots and bows or laid out in patterns and stitched in place.

▲ **Embroidery**
Machine embroidery can be heavily worked to "push back" an area or to create effective reflections or shadows.

▲ **Beads**
Anything from humorous buttons and glitzy sequins to the single tiny bead on the warrior's shield (above) can be used as surface embellishment.

techniques for pictorial quilts

WORKING OVER PAPERS in the so-called
English patchwork method and the
relatively new technique of
foundation piecing are common
methods of pictorial quiltmakers.
However, appliqué is the most
pertinent method for making pictures
in fabric because of its adaptability
and the relative ease of working
curved shapes. This chapter
concentrates on standard quilting
equipment and appliqué techniques.

Glory of the Deep (detail)
Hava Salter

Materials and Equipment

The equipment for making pictorial quilts is the same as that needed for quiltmaking in general. The specific tools required depend on the techniques used to create the piece of work. For patchwork, for example, you will probably use a rotary cutter, ruler, and mat; for appliqué you might only need scissors. There are dozens of specialized pieces of equipment that have been created or adapted for use by quiltmakers, and you might find it useful to experiment with some of them to discover if they speed up the labor-intensive processes. Because most pictorial quilts are unique – truly one of a kind – most quiltmakers will find their essential equipment in a sewing box, in a home workshop, or on a desk.

Chalk pencil

Lead pencil

Soapstone pencil

Transfer pencil

Silver quilter's pencil

Fade-away pencil

Water-soluble pen

Watercolor pencil

Tailor's pencil

Tailor's chalk

Tailor's wheel

Cardboard

Self-adhesive film

Freezer paper

▲ Marking equipment

You will need a selection of pens and pencils, for marking motifs and templates onto both cardboard and fabric. Bear in mind that some marks, such as lead pencil, seldom wash out of fabric and tailor's chalk rubs away quickly. There are many specialized pens available for the quilter: experiment to find your favorite.

Adjustable square

Compass

Protractor

Seam gauge

Tape measure

T-square

Flexible curve

Plastic ruler

◀ Measuring and drawing

Much of the drafting equipment, from ordinary rulers to a drawing compass or protractor, can be found on any desk. Specialized tools, such as a flexible curve or seam gauge, can be useful. Paper for drafting and making templates, including tracing paper, is essential.

▼ Sewing kit

A basic selection of sewing equipment should include needles (sharps for piecing and betweens for appliqué and quilting), straight pins, sewing thread in a variety of colors, and the thimble of your choice if you use one.

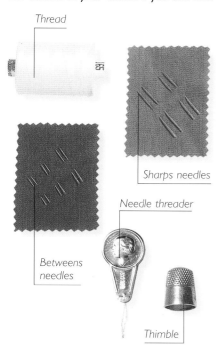

Thread

Sharps needles

Needle threader

Betweens needles

Thimble

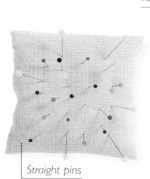

Straight pins

▶ Embellishments

Your sewing basket can become a treasure trove of items that can be used to embellish pictorial quilts. Beads and sequins come in a huge array of colors, sizes, and shapes. Shells and other found objects can add texture, and yarn and thread of all kinds can be incorporated. Keep things in separate containers for ease of access.

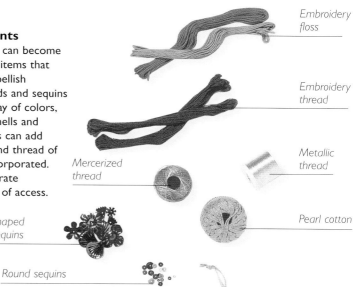

Embroidery floss

Embroidery thread

Metallic thread

Mercerized thread

Pearl cotton

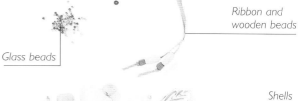

Shaped sequins

Round sequins

Ribbon and wooden beads

Glass beads

Shells

▶ Cutting

In addition to rotary cutting equipment for patchwork and for cutting borders and backing fabric, several pairs of scissors will be helpful, including a small sharp pair for cutting thread and clipping seam allowances, and separate pairs for cutting fabric and paper.

Thread scissors

Seam ripper

Paper scissors

Fabric scissors

Rotary ruler

Rotary cutter

Cutting mat

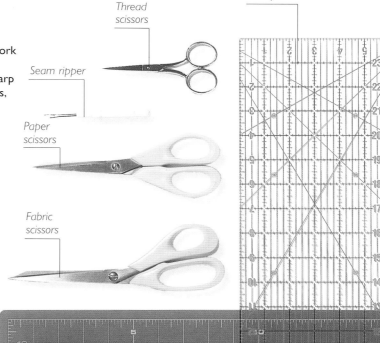

FUSIBLE WEBBING

Fusible webbing is a useful addition to the pictorial quilter's basic equipment. It is a thin adhesive film with a paper backing, which provides a quick and secure way to hold appliqué pieces in place. Pieces can be traced on the paper side and ironed onto the wrong side of fabric before being cut out. When the paper backing is removed, the other side of the webbing can be ironed onto the work. The bond is permanent, so work carefully. Remember, too, that the webbing creates another layer, thin but slightly rigid, that will always be in the piece of work, unlike other methods of holding pieces firm. However, it is ideal for securing small or narrow pieces of fabric.

There are several weights available. It is possible to stitch the ultralight version by hand or machine, but the heavier weights should be worked on the machine. The design will be reversed when the piece is ironed on the backing, so be careful when you are tracing around the motif.

Preparation

Because appliqué usually involves a variety of different shapes, you may need to make patterns and templates. Cutting out pieces for appliqué work can be more akin to dressmaking than to the rotary-cutting methods now used for patchwork, and it is useful to be familiar with both methods. Bias-cut strips are also useful for the pictorial quiltmaker.

Making templates

Pictorial shapes are often irregular, so a stiff template provides an easy way to mark the image on fabric so it can be cut out or stitched over. Any type of clean, fairly lightweight cardboard can be used.

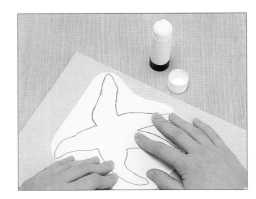

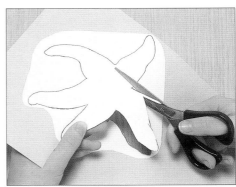

1 Draw or trace the image on paper (see page 20) – virtually any type of paper is suitable – and glue the paper to cardboard.

2 Using paper scissors, cut around the marked line carefully. You can use longer-lasting template plastic to make a template that will be used many times.

Cutting out with scissors

Cutting out can be done in several ways. You can cut around a line marked directly on the fabric, or make a paper pattern by drawing or tracing, or draw around a template. Be sure to include a seam allowance where necessary. Make sure your scissors are sharp and used either for paper and cardboard, or for fabric, whichever is appropriate for the method you are using.

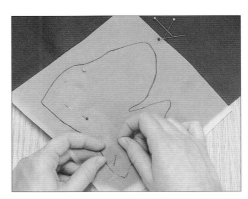

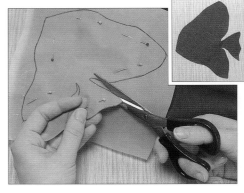

1 Draw or trace the motif on paper. Pin the pattern to the chosen fabric, making sure it is the right way up.

2 Cut out the motif using fabric scissors, working carefully around the marked line and avoiding the pins. *Inset:* Remove the paper. The motif is now ready to be used.

Rotary cutting

The rotary cutter and its companion ruler and self-healing mat have changed the way patchwork quilts are made. Strips and individual patches can be cut quickly and accurately using this method.

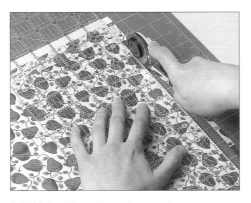

1 Fold the fabric along the straight grain to fit on the mat and place the ruler over the "good" fabric. Holding the ruler steady, cut away the uneven edge and discard it.

2 Turn the fabric so that the ruler covers the "good" area. Use either the ruler or the mat – not both – to align and measure the fabric. Cut strips of the desired width.

Cutting pieced strips

The speed of working with rotary-cut strips comes from the fact that they can be stitched together in a sequence and then cut again before being reassembled into different patterns.

1 Stitch strips together and press the seams to one side. Lay the pieced strip on the mat, align the ruler across it, and cut pieced strips of the desired width.

2 The procedure is the same if you wish to cut strips at an angle to the seams. Cut the end of the strip on the diagonal and measure from that edge.

Cutting a bias strip

Cutting bias strips of fabric can be accomplished with scissors, but is much quicker using rotary equipment. The technique is the same whether you are cutting strips along the straight grain or on the bias. Appliquéd bias strips should be cut three times wider than the line to be covered.

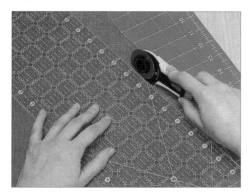

1 Lay the fabric on the cutting mat and with the ruler covering the "good" material, trim the edge along the width to make a straight line.

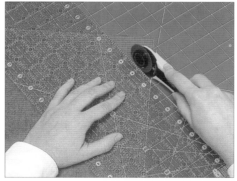

2 Measure a 45-degree angle on the ruler and cut off the corner of the fabric to give a short edge on the true bias.

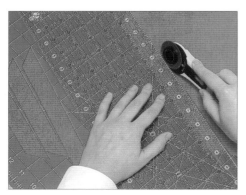

3 Using the edge cut in Step 2 as the guideline, cut strips of the desired width, always covering the good side of the fabric with the ruler.

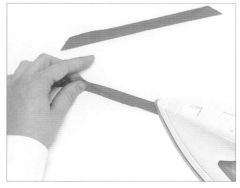

4 Most bias strips will be used as some form of binding, so press – do not iron – each strip in half lenghwise (see box). Do not stretch the strip out of shape as you work.

PRESSING

Pressing is a fundamental part of making any quilt, and a pictorial quilt is no exception. When you are joining patches, seams are normally pressed to one side, if possible toward the darker fabric to prevent show-through. Appliqué pieces are often pressed – on the wrong side if possible – to create a sharp crease for stitching, and several types of appliqué are based on pressing fusible webbing or iron-on interfacing to the wrong side of the fabric piece. A dry iron will not spatter, and a pressing cloth will prevent shine on fabrics with pile or a special finish.

Pressing means just that – never drag the iron along a seam, or you may stretch it out of shape.

Piecing

There are two ways of joining patchwork pieces – by hand and by machine. Hand-sewn piecing is usually more time-consuming, but should afford a great degree of accuracy, especially on curved seams and sharp-pointed edges, and be satisfying to anyone who enjoys manipulating fabric. Machine piecing is much quicker to work, particularly on pieces that need straight seams, and is ideal for quiltmakers with limited stitching time. Pictorial quilts are frequently assembled using some of each method.

Straight piecing by hand

Certain shapes are easier to stitch by hand, especially if they have sharp points or curved seams. The patches can be joined with a backstitch or a simple running stitch. Mark the seamline on the wrong side and pin or baste carefully.

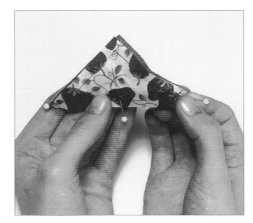

1 With right sides together, pin the shapes to be joined along the straight seam, matching the corners on each piece.

2 Sew along the marked seamline, beginning and ending precisely at the corners. Handle bias seams carefully to avoid stretching.

Four-piece seams by hand

Matching the seams where several corners meet is not difficult, but preparation should be done carefully. Avoid stitching in the seam allowances in case you need to clip or trim them later.

1 To make a four-patch block, join patches in pairs along the seamlines with a neat running stitch. Press the seams carefully in opposite directions.

2 Pin pairs of patches together, pushing a pin through the center seam to mark it precisely and then pinning along the seamline to the corners.

3 Working from the center out, join the patches with a running stitch. *Inset:* From the right side (left), the corners meet precisely in the middle.

English piecing

In this traditional method of hand piecing, fabric shapes are basted to backing papers cut to the correct size and shape and joined by sewing them together along the edge. The fabric shapes are marked on the wrong side and cut an approximate ¼ in (5 mm) larger than the backing papers. This technique is widely used for piecing hexagons and diamonds, as well as for curved shapes like clamshells.

1 Pin a backing paper to the wrong side of each fabric patch. Fold the seam allowance over the paper and baste the patch in place.

2 Level the edges of two patches, right sides together, and whipstitch them together through the fabric only. *Inset:* Set in the next piece and work from the center out.

Joining pieced units by machine

Strips that have been joined by machine and cut into short units can be joined quickly and accurately by machine. To reduce bulk, press the seams of each unit in opposite directions before joining them.

1 Place two units with right sides together and seams pressed in opposite directions. Align the seams and stitch ¼ in (5 mm) from the raw edge.

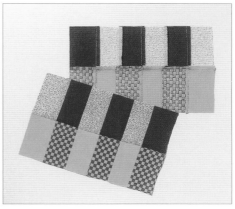

2 Joined units (front and back) have evenly matched rows with squared-off corners at each junction.

Stitching curved seams by machine

Careful preparation, marking, and pinning are all essential when you join curved patches by machine. The bias-cut seams need cautious handling to keep them from stretching. Mark the seamline on the wrong side of the fabric before you begin.

1 Pin the patches together, with the pins at right angles to the curved edge. Pin the center first, then each end, then in between as necessary.

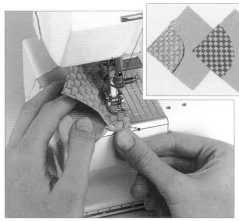

2 Stitch along the marked line, removing pins as you go. *Inset:* Pressing the seam toward the concave edge will help it to lie flat.

Hand Appliqué: Cut and Sew

The most basic form of appliqué is known as cut and sew, since that is just what you do. This type of applied work lends itself to simple shapes, and decorative stitching can be used to hold the pieces on the background fabric to great effect. Felt, as we have used here, works extremely well, but any fabric that does not fray can be used with equal success.

It is also possible to work cut-and-sew appliqué on ordinary woven fabric such as cotton or silk, especially if each piece is backed with a lightweight iron-on interfacing to keep the raw edges from unraveling.

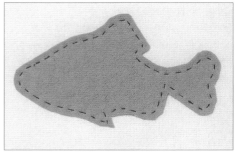

Simple shape
Felt comes in a multitude of bright colors that work well when you are making simple shapes, like this fish, sewn with running stitch.

1 Make templates and patterns for each motif. Pin each one to fabric of the appropriate color and cut them all out with fabric scissors.

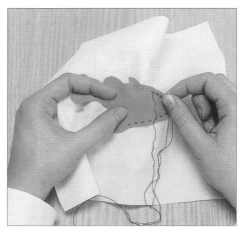

2 Using an appropriate decorative embroidery stitch, sew the shape to the background fabric. A book of embroidery stitches will have plenty of ideas.

3 Decorate or embellish the shape as you wish. *Inset:* Adding a sequin eye to this fish shape makes it much more realistic. Many other types of decoration can be used.

4 To make a picture panel, cut out all the shapes and arrange them on the background. Pin them in place.

5 Many different embroidery stitches can be used to attach the shapes. Here, we have used running stitch, backstitch, chain stitch, cross stitch, blanket stitch, herringbone stitch, fly stitch, and straight stitch, and a variety of embellishments — beads, sequins, and french knots — were used to make the eyes.

Hand Appliqué: Turned Edges

Perhaps the most familiar way of working appliqué is the method known as turned edges. The motif is cut out with a narrow seam allowance, which is then turned under as you slipstitch the shape in place on the background fabric. Some people simply pin the shape in place and turn as they sew, but most of us find it much easier to work accurately if the motif is basted in place on the background. Two of the most commonly used methods are shown here. Plain-weave fabrics are the best choice for turned-edge appliqué as blends and jersey do not turn under as readily.

Basted shape
The turned edges technique gives a smooth edge to the fabric shape.

1 Draw or trace the motif on paper. Glue the shape to cardboard and cut it out. On the right side of the fabric, draw around the cardboard shape lightly with a tailor's pencil.

2 Cut out the fabric shape carefully with fabric scissors, leaving an approximate ¼ in (5 mm) seam allowance all around the motif.

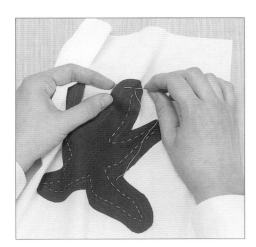

3 Using small stitches, baste the wrong side of the shape to the right side of the background fabric approximately ¼ in (5 mm) inside the marked line. Carefully trim the raw edges so they are about ¼ in (5 mm) outside the marked line.

4 Using the end of the needle, turn the raw edge under to abut the basted line, and slipstitch the shape to the background using matching thread. *Inset:* Remove the basting carefully and press the shape from the wrong side.

ALTERNATIVE TECHNIQUE

In this method a piece of fabric is basted to the background from the wrong side and then cut to shape.

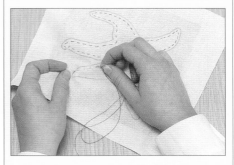

1 *Use the template to draw around the shape on the wrong side of the background fabric. Remember that the shape will appear in reverse on the right side. Cut a piece of fabric larger all around than the motif and use contrasting thread to baste it in place, right side up, on the right side of the background, but working from the wrong side, about ¼ in (5 mm) inside the drawn line.*

2 *Turn the piece to the right side and cut out the shape with fabric scissors, approximately ¼ in (5 mm) from the basted line. Proceed to work the shape as in Step 4 (left).*

Hand Appliqué: Plain Paper

Some shapes are easier to work if they are backed with something stiffer than the fabric while they are being applied. The traditional method for working awkwardly shaped patchwork patterns – hexagons and diamonds particularly – can be adapted to back pictorial motifs. It is also a good way of stabilizing thin fabrics such as voile or silk. Unlike the interfacing or fusible webbing used in some methods to firm up shapes, plain paper is removed from the final work, usually before the last stitching is done.

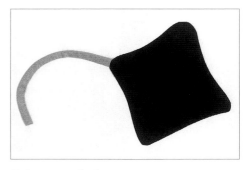

Diamond shape
The skate's body, adapted from a diamond shape, has been worked over paper for easier handling.

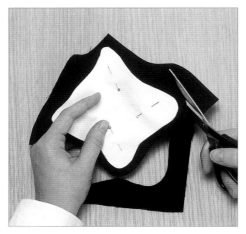

1 Draw or trace the motif on plain paper. Cut out each shape and pin to the chosen fabric. Cut out each piece, leaving a seam allowance [at least ¼in (5 mm)] all around.

2 Turn the seam allowance to the wrong side over the edge of the paper and baste it in place. Press the edge lightly with an iron from the wrong side if you wish.

3 Position the first piece on the background fabric and slipstitch in place using matching thread. Here, the first piece is the thin tail, made from a bias strip (*see box, right*). Pin the next piece – the body – to the background and slipstitch in place, covering up raw edges on the previous piece as you work.

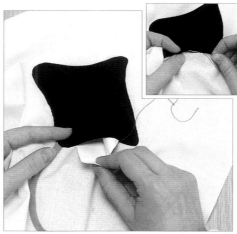

4 Leaving a gap large enough to remove the paper backing, take out the basting stitches and slip the backing paper out. *Inset:* Finish the slipstitching.

BIAS STRIPS
There are several methods for applying bias strips. The method below is the one that I use regularly.

1 *Cut a bias strip a little longer than necessary and 1½in (4 cm) wide. Press it in half lengthwise, wrong sides together. Do not iron it – this will stretch it. Pin the strip in place on the background.*

2 *Stitch in place along the center of the strip using small running stitches. Ease the strip around curves gently, being careful not to stretch it. Trim the raw edges approximately ⅛in (3 mm) from the stitching line.*

3 *Turn the doubled strip over the stitched line and slipstitch it in place along the folded edge.*

4 *Turn under any ends that will show and slipstitch them down. Ends that will be covered by another piece can be left unfinished.*

Hand Appliqué: Freezer Paper

Freezer paper is a special plastic-coated paper, originally designed to wrap food, especially fresh meat, for freezing. It is a boon to appliqué work because the paper side can be drawn on, and the shiny plastic side can be ironed onto the wrong side of fabric to stabilize it. The raw edges are turned under and basted down through the paper as in the paper-piecing method, giving an equally firm edge to stitch. However, because the paper sticks to the fabric, it is generally easier to work small pieces. It can be reused several times, making it especially useful when you are repeating motifs across a quilt.

Intricate shape
With small, intricate shapes the paper can be removed through a small hole cut in the background fabric.

1 Trace each element of the design separately on the paper side. Remember to reverse the design or the motif will be the wrong way around. Cut out each piece and iron it on the wrong side of the chosen piece of fabric.

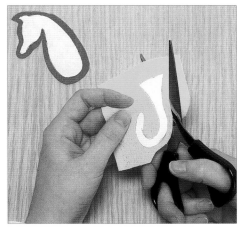

2 Cut around the paper shape, leaving an approximate ¼ in (5 mm) seam allowance all around. Repeat to cut out all the shapes in sequence.

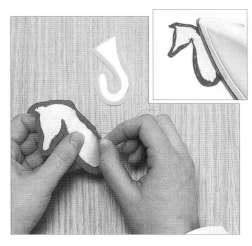

3 Turn the raw edges to the wrong side and baste in place. Clip into the seam allowance to ease the turning where necessary. *Inset:* Press the edges down with an iron to make a crisper fold if you wish.

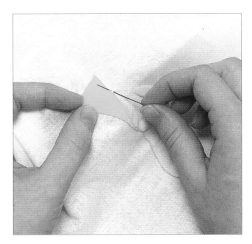

4 Position the first piece on the background fabric and pin it in place. Slipstitch all around the piece using matching thread. Leave an opening in a logical place so that you can remove the paper.

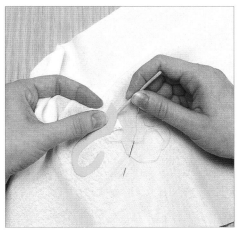

5 Here, the top of the tail will be hidden under the body, so it can be left open. Remove the paper. This raw edge will be covered by the next piece so there is no need to turn it under.

6 Apply the next piece the same way. Begin in a place that will make it easier to leave an opening through which to remove the paper, and finish stitching after the paper has been removed.

Hand Appliqué: Reverse Appliqué

Reverse appliqué is a somewhat specialized technique, but one that can be used very effectively in pictorial quilts. It is used to build up layers of contrasting fabric, so the resulting work is at least two layers thick, and usually more. Entire quilts can be made this way, or separate sections can be incorporated into other forms of appliqué and patchwork.

It is the technique used by stitchers on the San Blas Islands of Panama to make their traditional molas – panels of reverse appliqué that are incorporated into garments and bags, or used as wall hangings. It works well for simple shapes, such as the fish here, and comes into its own with intricate patterns, such as small, multicolored individual feathers on a bird's wing or scales on a snake's body.

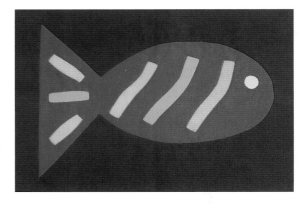

Multicolored layers

Three layers of lightweight cotton – dark blue on top, then turquoise followed by orange – have been used here. The eye is made from a separate yellow scrap inserted after the main body has been sewn to help reduce bulk and save fabric.

1 Cut out pieces to make layers of fabric. Draw the main pattern on the top piece and baste all the layers together ¼ in (5 mm) outside the marked line.

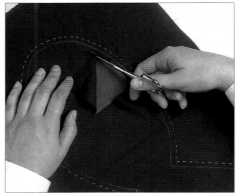

2 Snip the first layer carefully and cut away the main shape ¼ in (5 mm) inside the marked line. Make sure you do not cut through any of the subsequent layers.

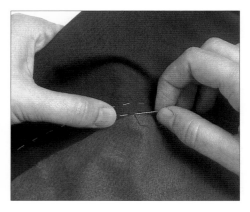

3 Turn under the seam allowance to abut the basted line and slipstitch the raw edges in place all around the shape. If possible, stitch through the second layer only.

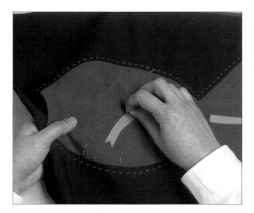

4 Draw the patterns for the next layer and baste as before. Working the same way, cut away the shapes in the second layer of fabric and slipstitch the edges.

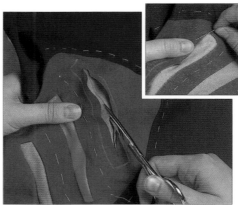

5 Cut out the designs in the third layer the same way. Always be very careful not to cut through the subsequent layer. *Inset:* Continue slipstitching the elements in the third layer until the design is complete.

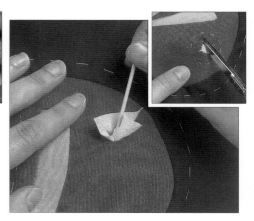

6 Cut a small opening for the eye. Insert a scrap large enough to cover the area and baste it in place as before. *Inset:* Clip the allowance; then slipstitch the raw edges and remove the basting.

Hand Appliqué: Shadow Appliqué

Shadow appliqué is a particularly useful technique for pictorial quiltmakers, softening colors and giving the impression of depth. Depending on the desired effect, any sheer fabric can be used, from the silk organza shown here to net, tulle, or gauze. Use bold deep colors behind the sheer layer; they will show through better than pastels. Embellishments can be added to the piece either before or after the sheer layer has been applied. It all depends on the look you wish to achieve.

Sheer shapes

Using a contrasting thread to join the two layers highlights the shape underneath the sheer fabric.

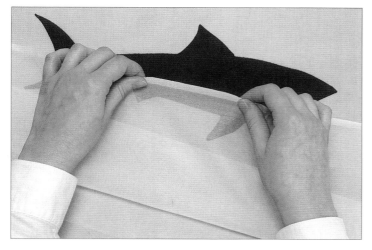

1 Apply the shape to the background fabric using an appropriate method. We used the freezer paper technique (see page 45). Cut a piece of organza or net, large enough to cover the required area and place it over the shape.

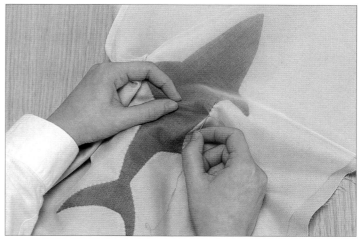

2 Lay the organza over the appliqué and work around the outline of the shape with a small running stitch. This both secures the organza and acts as an embellishment.

PEAKS AND VALLEYS

Also known as points and troughs. Most appliqué pieces have at least one sharp point and a corresponding dip. There are a few tricks that make it easier to work them neatly.

Valleys

A valley, or trough, or dip, can be sharp or shallow. To work pointed dips, press back the raw edges and clip – as you approach it – the seam allowance at the lowest point. Shallower curves can be clipped in several places, again as you reach the spot, not in advance, to keep the line smooth.

Valley

Trough

Peaks

Points are tricky to work because they inevitably have a surplus of fabric in the seam allowance that must be removed – very carefully – if at all possible. Curved "hills" can have notches removed to make it easier to turn the allowance under. Removing the tip of a sharp peak as shown will facilitate turning under a neat point.

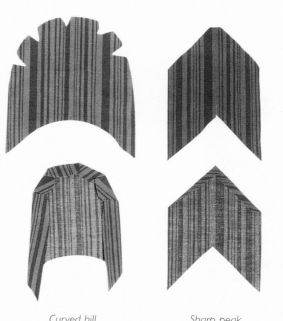

Curved hill

Sharp peak

Hand Appliqué: Stained Glass

This appliqué technique can be used to create attractive shapes with an outline that gives the effect of a piece of stained glass. The outlining is worked using narrow strips of bias-cut fabric. Traditionalists may wish to make their own, especially if a particular color is desired (see page 39), but it is also possible to use ordinary narrow purchased bias binding, or to buy lengths of bias strip with an iron-on backing, made especially for the purpose, as shown here. The bias strips can be stitched in place by hand or machine. A similar effect can be derived by working satin stitch (see page 51) around the shapes if you wish.

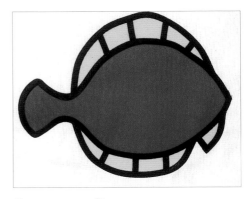

Strong outlines

Each yellow fin was drawn as one piece and then cut apart individually to indicate the placement of the bias strips.

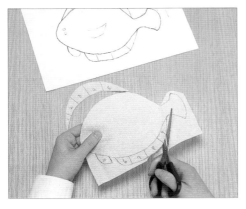

1 Trace the pattern on the paper side of lightweight fusible webbing and cut out all the pieces. Remember that the design will be reversed on the finished piece.

2 Iron all the pieces to the wrong side of the chosen fabrics and cut each one out. I have numbered each fin piece to avoid confusion. No seam allowances are necessary because all the edges will be covered by the bias strips.

3 Peel the backing paper off the main piece and iron the shape onto the background fabric. Remember that fusible webbing will not wash out.

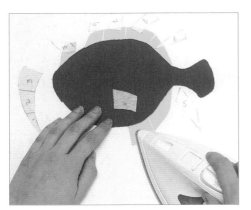

4 Iron on all the other pieces, working in sequence. Do not remove the backing paper until you are ready to iron that particular piece in place.

5 Apply the bias strips. Wherever possible cover raw ends with subsequent strips – here the short fin pieces were worked first. Iron or baste each strip in sequence and slipstitch or zigzag stitch each one in place. The iron-on backing will wash out, so it must be secured.

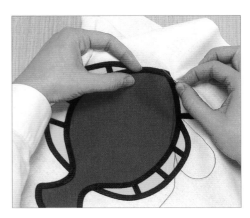

6 Finish all the bias-covered edges, working around the body last to cover all the raw edges. Because the final end is cut on the bias, it will not fray, but it can be secured with a few small stitches.

Machine Appliqué

The sewing machine is a useful tool for applied work, capable of creating fine, interesting results. You need, at the very least, a machine with a zigzag stitch function and many modern machines have built-in decorative embroidery stitches that can be used to outline and embellish machine appliqué work to good effect. Always make a test swatch before embarking on a piece of work to make sure that the stitch length and width are suitable. If you have an open embroidery or appliqué foot, it will be easier to see what is happening as you work.

There are several ways to hold pieces in place as you stitch around them. Pinning and basting are not usually suitable for machine work. Using basting spray or craft glue means the piece can be repositioned, and the adhesive washes out. Fusible webbing, used on page 48, creates a permanent bond.

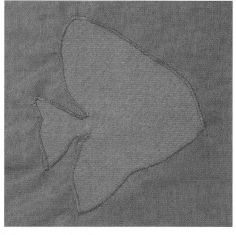

Zigzag stitch

Basting spray is an aerosol fabric glue that creates a firm but temporary bond, which holds the shape on the background. A decorative stitch, such as zigzag stitch, can then be applied.

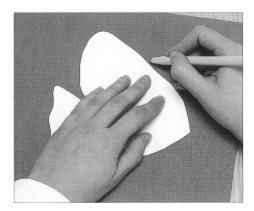

1 Make templates for each piece of the design. Pieces for machine appliqué do not need seam allowances; the stitching is done along the raw edges. Draw around each piece on the chosen fabric. Make sure that the template is the right way up, or the piece will be reversed. Cut out all the pieces.

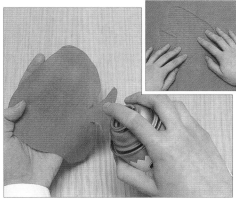

2 Spray the wrong side of the piece to be applied with a light coating of basting spray. *Inset:* Position the shape on the background fabric.

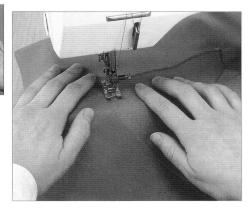

3 Set the machine for the desired stitch and do a test. Begin stitching in a place that can be covered by another piece or hidden by the stitching. Work around the shape using your chosen stitch.

BRODERIE PERSE

Broderie perse is the name given to a style of appliqué in which motifs are cut from a printed fabric and stitched to a different background.

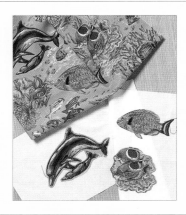

1 Decide on the motifs you like and cut them out. Choose shapes that have enough clean lines to work with – too many complicated areas can be impossible to stitch.

2 You can use any of the methods in this section to apply the motif to the background, depending on the weight and weave of the fabric, the effect you wish to create, and the use to which the finished piece will be put.

Decorative Stitches and Embellishments

Most pictorial quilts will be enhanced by the use of various forms of embellishment once the basic design has been stitched. Quilting, surface embroidery, decorative outlining, and found objects can all be used to add texture and liveliness to the finished piece. The choice of decoration is limited only by the maker's imagination and resourcefulness. Anything that can be attached in some way – usually but not necessarily by stitching – can be used in any way that is felt to be appropriate to the subject and execution of the work. The main danger of embellishment is the possibility of overworking the piece – learning to edit your selection is the key. The ideas shown here are only a small selection of the endless possibilities at your disposal. Instructions for making these stitches can be found in any book on embroidery.

French knots

French knots are one of the most useful embroidery stitches for embellishing pictorial quilts. Here they depict the knobbly areas on the body of a starfish, but they – along with their cousins, bullion knots – have many other uses, such as to create massed blooms in a flowerbed, for example.

Outlining

Outlining has the effect of making a shape stand out from the elements around it. Motifs can be outlined, either inside the shape or out, with a decorative embroidery or quilting stitch. If the outlining can be used as part of the assembly process as well, as here where it is used to anchor the shape to the background, so much the better. However, remember that this technique works best on nonfray fabrics.

French knots could be used to hold a ribbon in place as well as being decorative.

Elongated french knots

This seahorse sports a bead eye and a stem stitch mouth as well as his textured tail. The elongated variation of french knots serves as a good outline stitch with a myriad of uses.

Beads

Beads come in all shapes, sizes, and colors, and because they are so versatile, they rank among the pictorial quiltmaker's best friends. Here two tiny green beads have been used to make the skate's eyes. French knots have been used again on the body and tail.

Straight stitch

The gills on this shark's body have been worked in straight stitch, using thread the same color as the body, which is covered with a shadow layer of silk organza. This toning of color is a good way to enhance a shape without garishness.

The mouth is an elongated fly stitch.

Sequins

Like beads, sequins are wonderfully useful and add not just texture but a sparkle as well. They often work well as eyes, as in this example, and can be sewn with either side facing up to achieve different effects.

The body fin is made from the same binding that was used to outline the shapes.

Satin stitch

Satin stitch is one of the most effective outline stitches whether it is worked by hand or machine, as it is here. Machine satin stitch, really a close zigzag, is the stitch used most often for machine appliqué because it makes a clean outline and covers raw edges securely. A starburst sequin has been used for the eye.

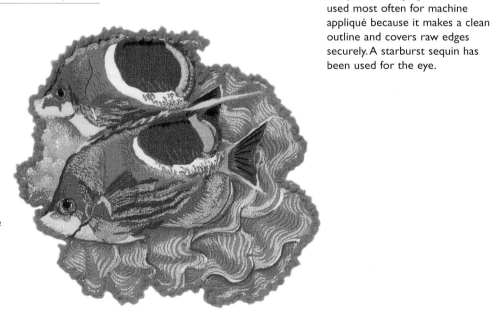

Cording

Another effective way of adding texture while hiding raw edges is to cover them with an outline of cording using an appropriate decorative thread, yarn, braid, or cord. This textured wool yarn gives a bubbly edge to this broderie perse motif.

pictorial themes

SELECTING A THEME for a pictorial quilt is a highly personal choice, and literally anything that can be portrayed realistically is a possibility. Landscapes, people and places, flora and fauna are among the most obvious starting places for anyone who wishes to design and stitch a pictorial quilt. All these themes are discussed in the sections that follow.

land and sea

AMONG THE MOST popular themes for pictorial quilts are landscapes and seascapes. The atmosphere that can be evoked in a picture of a house or a bridge or a rocky beach or a desert landscape provides quiltmakers with a thought-provoking challenge that many cannot resist.

Like a Brook out of a River of Mighty Waters
Tottie Parmeter

African Landscape

Making a quilt to commemorate a particular place is a way to evoke memories – of a trip-of-a-lifetime, a beloved spot closer to home, or a favorite view, perhaps. Choosing images that call to mind feelings associated with a special place can be a process of elimination, since one or two strong symbols will provide a flash of recognition that may be lost if the design is too complicated.

By incorporating the setting sun into the English paper-pieced background, this quiltmaker, who loves travel and nature in equal measure, has given herself a canvas for two images – a crane in flight and an ancient, sculptural tree – that to her say, "That's Africa." The resulting starkness is a counterpoint to the richness of the chosen colors.

▼ **Sunset in Africa**
Silvia Momesso Ranieri
PAPER PIECING, HAND QUILTING

The quiltmaker's family manufactured silk ties, and she uses recycled silk more than any other material. The bright colors of the fabrics and the rich texture created by the hand quilting convey, as much as the severity of the images themselves, the feeling of vast wilderness associated with the African continent.

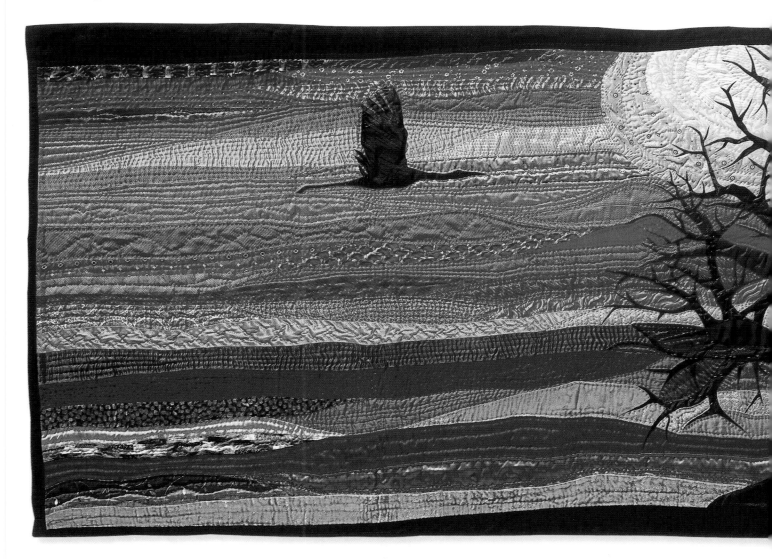

▼ Bird in flight
The upstretched wings above the long thin body of the flying crane are made from carefully positioned strips of dark blue silk.

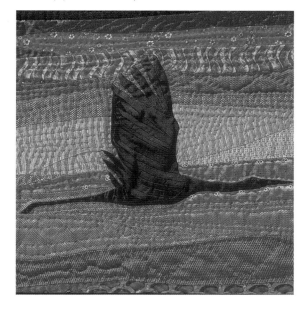

▲ Tree of life
The leafless tree has an anthropomorphic shape that evokes a feeling of welcome from Mother Earth, while the spiky branches warn of possible dangers in the unknown lands beyond.

The subtle blending of colors in the background makes it difficult to discern the exact location of the horizon, exactly as we might expect at sunset.

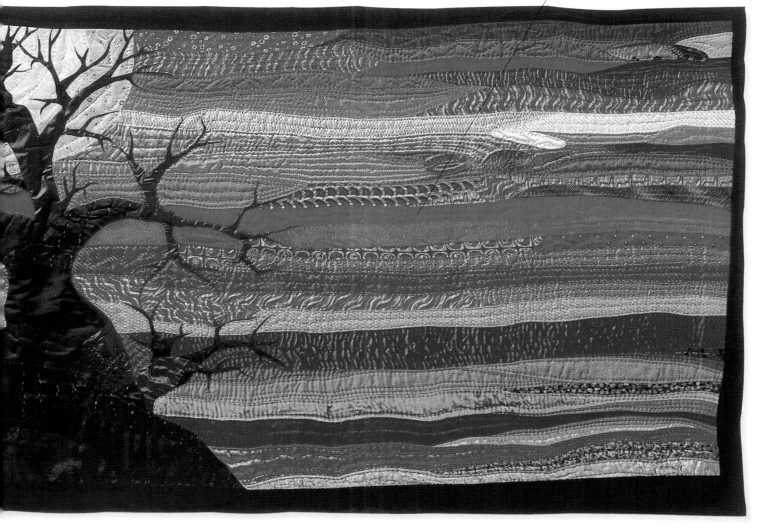

Lateral Links

Creating a specific pictorial effect in a fabric landscape, such as a sense of perspective, is a challenge that appeals to many pictorial quiltmakers. Altering the traditional approach to applying a particular technique often requires a certain amount of lateral thinking but means that exciting new results can occur in unexpected ways.

Carefully color-graded rows of Flying Geese can be used to create a varied and striking background, for instance, or strips of simple Prairie Points can form the branches of a pine tree. Traditional leaf or flower blocks can be incorporated into a picture of a garden or conservatory, while mosaic patterns can be transformed into floors, paths, or walls.

▶ **Beyond the Dragon Gate** Kate Molloy
MACHINE PIECING, APPLIQUE, HAND EMBROIDERY, HAND QUILTING

Working a pictorial quilt can offer an excellent exercise in lateral thinking. Using tried-and-tested techniques in a non-traditional way can create highly effective impressions. Here, Flying Geese strips in a variety of sizes are worked in a "watercolor" arrangement, in which the colors are graded according to their values (see page 27) to make the land portions of this scene. The paler water areas are also pieced watercolor-style, but from diamond-shaped strips, while the sky is a single piece of painted fabric. The slight sheen of the upholstery fabrics used contributes to the overall feel of the piece.

▶ **Looking ahead**
The fretwork at the top and bottom of the scene is made from strips of ribbon applied to the finished background. The quilting, both the lines of stitches and the tufts of tied quilting, is worked by hand using metallic thread.

The piece, one of a related pair, is hung from loops of cord that are visible along the top.

The sky is quilted with random ties, giving the area an entirely different feel from the land and water. Tying has also been used to quilt the border.

The elegant bridge is made from thin bias strips cut from upholstery fabric.

The pale reflection of the bridge in the calm water below has been embroidered with long hand stitches worked in a dark metallic thread.

Textured Towers

Texture is all-important in pictorial quilts. The fabrics selected play an important part in the textural interest that a piece provides, but the quilting itself is crucial. Minimal stitching can be used to outline particular areas to highlight them and make them appear more important, or dense quilting can fill spaces to give a specific impression. Heavy quilting is more effective on plain fabric than it is on prints, where the stitches tend to get lost in the pattern.

> *I based this piece on a painting by Paul Klee entitled* **Kathedrale.**
>
> Christine Shaw

▶ To View the Domes and Towers with Klee
Christine Shaw
BONDED APPLIQUE, BIG-STITCH QUILTING

Four layers of dyed cheesecloth (muslin) were placed on a layer of yellow cotton fabric, and a mixture of silk, cotton, and metallic fabrics were bonded to this background. After the bonded shapes were anchored in place with straight machine stitch, they were hand quilted with big stitches to delineate each space.

The background layers of cheesecloth were slashed through to expose all the colors, and the exposed raw edges add another level of texture to the piece.

Straight-line stitching has been worked everywhere except in the curves of the large red dome (top right).

▲ Greetings from Gafsa

Margaret Ramsay

PATCHWORK, MACHINE QUILTING

Buildings in this Tunisian town are reproduced from a watercolor sketch, made in satin and heavily quilted. Windows are shuttered, plants grow in courtyards, vines climb up walls. Because each differently colored area has its own particular quilting pattern, each is immediately discernible and as recognizable as the satellite dish on top of the central house.

Two identical doors, one half hidden by another building, have fanlights and geometric details, as well as hand symbols. The wall around the doors is densely textured, while the wall of the building behind is much less heavily worked.

◀ Pattern on plain fabric

A myriad of patterns has been used to differentiate between the disparate areas, giving a feel of layers and layers of buildings constructed higgledy-piggledy throughout the city. The excellent use of light and dark color values contributes greatly to the overall effect.

Remains of the Day

Evoking a particular time of day is an important part of creating a landscape quilt. The choice of colors and even fabrics will depend on whether you want to convey dawn, or sunset, or perhaps high noon, or even nighttime. The pink and orange hues of sunrise and sunset are very different from the bright blue of midday or the deep indigo of midnight. The effect of clouds or reflections from the sea will also alter the perception of time through the use of color.

> " *I felt it was appropriate to use vintage kimono fabrics for the 'torii' – the shrine – and the sun.* "
>
> **Jenni Dobson**

▼ Shinto Sunrise Jenni Dobson
PATCHWORK, MACHINE QUILTING, MACHINE EMBROIDERY

The background and borders are pieced with an eye to the overall color effect. "Threadplay," a layered machine-embroidery technique devised by Libby Lehman, has been worked using different colored metallic threads to make the sun's rays and the reflections.

The space-dyed fabric by Nancy Crow creates a pattern reminiscent of evening clouds being pierced by the last rays of the sun.

The fine stripe in the fabric used to make the "torii" reinforces the feeling of a wooden shrine. It has been worked by machine in a reverse appliqué technique.

The layers of stitching that make up the reflections in the water are painterly and highly effective.

▲ **Navajo Country** Pamela Foxall
PATCHWORK, PIECING, APPLIQUE

The landforms and the daytime sky of the background have been pieced and the pictorial elements applied on top. The scale lacks realism – some of the yellow flowers are as large as the treetops – but the piece evokes a strong feeling of time and place.

The figure in the bottom center is a Navajo symbol that adds greatly to the overall effect of the quilt.

The middle border is pieced from rectangles and squares to create a strongly geometric Native American pattern.

Places of Refuge

A pictorial quilt, like a painting, can convey a mood or impart a feeling. These two landscapes, very different in what they portray and in technique, both nonetheless emanate a sense of calm and contemplation. Other pieces on similar subjects might show energy and liveliness, frustration, or sadness. As always, the choice of color and fabric, as well as the point of view and the basic lines of the image, plays an important part in the creation of an overall effect.

A wood-grain fabric is mitered at the corners to make a realistic frame, with a piped "mat" between it and the picture.

▲ **A Calm Anchorage** Betty Cameron
APPLIQUE, SHADOW APPLIQUE, EMBROIDERY

The horizontal lines of the scene contribute to its serenity, as does the muting of the colors by the use of shadow appliqué. Subtle prints have been used in various places, such as the water and some of the trees, while a bright-colored flower pattern has been used to make the blooming areas.

▶ **Stitching on the shadows**
The piece is appliquéd in strong basic colors and covered with a layer of tulle net. Hand embroidery is used to outline and emphasize selected areas.

▼ The Barn Church Deborah Fife

PATCHWORK, MACHINE QUILTING, EMBROIDERY

The Barn Church, a landmark in southwest London where the maker lives, is adapted from a Barn block, similar to a House block, published in 1997. It was made as a raffle prize to raise money for the church. The choice of fabrics works extremely well, and the embroidered weathervane adds a delightful naive touch.

The gold flecks in the wide, deep blue border echo the stars in the darkening sky. The same fabric is used for the two small windows.

The barn's use as a church is denoted by the small Maltese cross shape embroidered below the window.

Three different beige/brown prints have been used to good effect to create the walls and door.

The pattern of a blue check fabric gives the impression of roof tiles in shadow and delineates the area from the similar color of the sky.

Anchors Aweigh

Ships at sea, with their billowing sails and multicolored hulls, provide a rich variety of pleasing shapes for the pictorial quiltmaker. Other motifs associated with the ocean, such as lighthouses, anchors, knotted ropes, and underwater life forms, have also been popular since picture and story quilts were first made.

Depicting the ocean's surface and the sky above offers scope for using a variety of techniques, from piecing strips of multicolored fabric to hand dyeing or painting, while the choice of colors and patterns for making boats and ships is endless, from traditional white to stripes and checks, and prints of all kinds.

The background fabric – an antique map pattern – has been carefully pieced here to create a "globe," to which the Mariner's Compass with its Cathedral Window center has been applied.

Pieces of thin rope have been positioned to form two favorite sailor's knots – the square or reef knot on the left and the clove hitch on the right – and couched in place on the wide inner border.

▶ **Sail Away** Sarah Hadfield
PATCHWORK, MACHINE APPLIQUE, MACHINE QUILTING

Fourteen sailing boats sashed in red surround a red-and-white striped lighthouse flashing its friendly hand-stitched beacon. Only five basic patterns are used to make the boats, but because each block is worked in different colors and some have been reversed, they all look completely different.

▲ Sea Fever Sally Holman
PATCHWORK, APPLIQUE, HAND QUILTING, MACHINE QUILTING, EMBROIDERY

This jolly piece, with its tall ship viewed through a Mariner's Compass porthole and surrounded by nautical motifs, is a seafarer's dream. The light blue sky contrasts dramatically with the rolling deep blue sea made of strips, and the reds and oranges in the compass and the corner stars echo the colors of the vessel.

◄ Sails aloft
The red sails, made separately and positioned in a realistic fashion along the masts, are made even more believable by the thread rigging.

Down to the Sea

Seascapes afford the pictorial quiltmaker endless possibilities for color, technique, and fabric. To these can be added equally infinite alternatives for embellishment to decorate the surface, such as the full complement of embroidery stitches; beads, shells, sequins, and feathers; and all manner of found materials. Further decoration can be added by quilting, either by hand or machine, in lightly or heavily worked simple patterns or outlining. Intricate seafaring motifs, trapunto and cording, or meandering lines will create texture to enhance the final effect.

▼ **Sail Free** Annie Taylor
APPLIQUE, HAND QUILTING

Are the boats lifting themselves out of the water and becoming birds, or are the seabirds touching the water and being transformed into boats? The superb color placement of the background strips delineates the darkening sky, the setting sun, and the reflections in the sea, and the simple machine quilting gives an overall liveliness and sense of realism to a beautifully conceived and executed piece of work.

The fully metamorphosed birds have close-quilted wings that give the impression of both feathers and flight.

Each boat has its embroidered ID number, in exactly the same place as the birds' eyes.

Curved lines of quilting on the background change shape slightly to denote clouds in the sky, hills, and ocean waves.

► Postcards of Home
Sally Holman
**PATCHWORK, APPLIQUE,
HAND QUILTING,
MACHINE QUILTING**

This clever quilt is based on a traditional Double Wedding Ring design. Each of the centers inside the rings is a window containing a portion of a seascape – sky in the top row, ocean and ships below, the water's edge, and the beach with its population of seabirds at the bottom. The muted colors used for the beautifully pieced rings, the linking squares, and the melon-shaped pieces echo sand, sea, and sky.

The touches of yellow and red in the boats complement the dark blue sea on which each sails.

▲ Shell seekers
Some of the shells on the printed fabric have been outline-quilted and stuffed, and the sand-colored strips that comprise the beach areas are embellished with real shells, beads, and french knots.

Beads and french knots have been used to good effect in a number of unexpected places in the areas depicting the beach.

◄ On the beach
As the scene moves inland – toward the viewer – more detail can be seen and identified. Birds and plants have been applied and embroidered, stones have been stuffed, and tiny flowers have been stitched in the sand to give a realistic effect.

Mountain Range

The splendor and drama of a mountainscape offer a variety of exciting challenges for the quilter. Both scale and perspective need to be considered and a careful selection of fabrics made to portray the different facets of the mountain slopes.

Upland scenery may also contain a great lake or river, and creating realistic reflections in a pictorial quilt is an interesting undertaking. Not only do the rules of perspective and other design considerations have to be carefully thought through for the view being depicted, but the same principles have to apply to the reflections, and in reverse. Select colors for the reflection that are a subdued version of the original.

▶ **Mount Shuksan-Shalom** Karen Schoepflin Hagen
PATCHWORK, APPLIQUE, HAND QUILTING

Shuksan is a mountain in North Cascades National Park in Washington state. The reflection of its tree-clad lower slopes and dazzling patches of snow appears on the surface of Picture Lake below.

▶ **Snow-topped summit**
The choice of fabrics used to depict the distant mountaintop and its year-round snow is wonderful, with silvery specks of sunlight and deep blue shadows.

◀ **Tall trees**
The realistic shape and color of the tree trunks and branches is highlighted by the appliquéd leaves with their frayed, feathery edges.

flowers and foliage

THEMES OF FLOWERS, foliage, and fruit and vegetables are among the most popular of all subjects for the pictorial quiltmaker. There are many floral images to choose from, and fabrics patterned with plants, of which there is an astonishing choice, can add to the overall visual texture of most quilts, especially those that depict garden themes.

Remembering Monet
Eileen B. Sullivan

In the Garden

Garden plants can be interpreted using all the methods in the quiltmaker's repertoire, from machine-stitched edges to shadow appliqué that looks like rainwater glistening on a leaf. The shading that can be achieved when hand dyeing and hand printing fabrics, can give a beautiful impression of light and shadow falling among leaves and flowers of varying tints and intensity. Painting fabric by hand opens an enormous range of possibilities, from hand-colored backgrounds to individual motifs.

> *Chinese lanterns grow in all my flowerbeds and look very cheerful. The quilt grew from an exercise to use as a teaching aid in a class about combining dyeing and printing and using graded color – from yellow to orange – in an exhibition quilt.*

Ann Israel

The leaves were appliquéd in place, then the zigzag stems were stitched and extended to make the central vein in each leaf.

The flowers have been placed to indicate the growth of the plant from its small buds to the fully-formed lanterns at the end of the season.

▶ **Chinese Lanterns**
Ann Israel
HAND DYEING AND PRINTING, APPLIQUE, QUILTING

The hand-printed leaves are appliquéd to a hand-dyed background that has been quilted using shapes that echo the calyxes of the Chinese lantern plant, or *Physalis*. The lanterns were created from hand-dyed fabrics left in an orange dye bath for varying lengths of time.

▼ Munching Molluscs Jill Packer

PATCHWORK, APPLIQUE, MACHINE QUILTING

The invertebrates of the title of this prize-winning quilt have eaten not only the maker's hosta leaves but have clearly made holes in the quilt itself – or someone has. The use of the Snail's Trail patchwork blocks as the background fabric is an effective and appropriate insider's joke that any quilter will appreciate.

I am plagued with snails in my garden … my paths are covered with silver snails' trails.

Jill Packer

▲ Spider's web
The machine-stitched web radiates out from the center of the piece, unifying the multicolored background and linking the ground-level hostas and their attackers with the taller plants, which are apparently just as desirable to the ever-hungry snails.

▶ Snail and leaf
The snail slithers away, leaving a chewed hosta leaf or two behind. The patchwork blocks, spider's web, and meander quilting were worked before the leaves, stems, and snails were appliquéd into position. Tiny dots of silver fabric paint are used to represent the snails' sticky trails.

A Receding View

Perspective in a landscape can be created in a number of ways. Making things appear smaller as they recede toward the horizon is one widely used method; creating a number of different levels is another. Careful arrangement of lights and darks to make areas of sunshine and shadow is also an effective approach that can be combined with other visual tricks to create a believable effect. Detail in the foreground, such as quilted leaves or flowers, adds to a sense of depth.

Elements within a landscape can also be positioned according to their size to enhance perspective. Trees in the woods or clouds in a sky can all be graduated to impart a feeling of realism, representing things to the eye as they might occur in real life.

▶ **Wistman's Wood** Diana Brockway
PIECING, APPLIQUE, MACHINE QUILTING, MACHINE EMBROIDERY

The curves in the background of this woodland piece do not diminish in size as they might in a traditional landscape, but the areas of light and dark, the texture created by the quilting that follows the contours, the gnarled central branch that recedes visually into the thicket, and the embellished deep border all contribute to the overall effect of a view seen through a window.

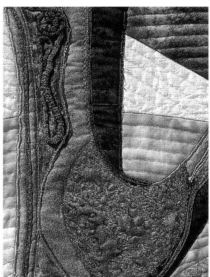

◀ **A mossy trunk**
This tree must face north, if the large patch of velvety moss in the crook of the branch, heavily embellished with machine embroidery, is a reliable indicator. The worms that have burrowed into the trunk are corded embroidery.

◀ **3D ferns**
The leaves on the lower border have been hand printed using a real fern, and either cut out and applied separately or outlined with metallic machine embroidery thread. The leaves along the top are both simple outlines and three-dimensional cutouts with machine satin-stitched stems.

▲ **Textured trunks**
The tree trunks and branches are all made from velvet. They have been appliquéd to the background and embellished with cording and embroidery using a variety of interesting novelty threads.

Floral Shapes

A pictorial quilt can be composed of one simple image, or it can be elaborate, containing many elements. Flowers offer the quilter a variety of shapes with which to work, from the simple tulip to a complicated bouquet. To achieve the desired impact, plan your selection carefully, especially when you are trying to place several elements into a cohesive context.

Even if you feel that your artistic skills are limited, it is important to begin with a visual reference. Simply make a rough sketch of your basic idea, and its elements will give you a starting point. Trace images (see page 20) that appeal to you and put them together with tape or glue until you have a plan.

▼ **Strong Inspirations** Vee Wilson
APPLIQUE, BRODERIE PERSE

The strong perspective in this formal garden is created in several ways, especially by the use of the vanishing point with its central focus – a tower – just below the horizon, and by the diminishing scale of the trees behind the main hedge.

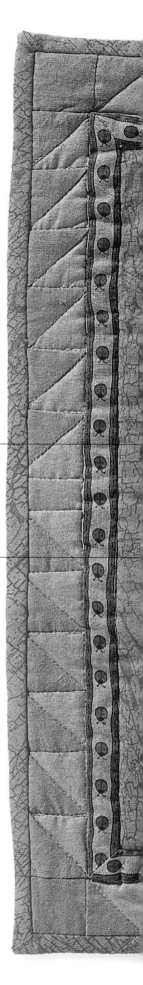

The insect fabric has been toned down by dyeing it in tea and turned to the wrong side to make the backs of the spiky wilted leaves.

The maker cut up a full-size drawing to make her pattern and used the paper-piecing method to assemble the hand-sewn quilt.

The same striped fabric has been used in the foreground and behind the low box hedge, but the perception is that the stripes in the distance are farther apart.

The massed bouquet of upholstery-fabric flowers in the cut-velvet urn is worked in broderie perse.

▶ **How Does Your Garden Grow? It Doesn't!**
Margaret Syrett
PATCHWORK, MACHINE QUILTING

Made for a "challenge" among the members of a local quilt group, this piece is a fine example of a well-conceived and constructed simple idea. Each participant had to use the insect fabric and work on a garden theme. The parched-earth feel of the background fabric adds to the sympathy the viewer feels for the poor dead plant, which has clearly not survived in spite of the files of ladybugs marching around the border.

Abundant Texture

Texture on pictorial quilts can be created in many ways. It can come from the surface stitching as well as from the alignment of the various elements within the design. Texture can be mainly visual, with the picture worked in two planes, or it can be three-dimensional. Stuffing, folding, ruching, and manipulating are all techniques that will add another dimension to pictures in fabric and are ideal for creating realistic vegetables.

► **Lunch M'Lady** Patricia Allen
APPLIQUE, HAND QUILTING, TRAPUNTO, EMBROIDERY

The wheelbarrow, appliquéd in hand-dyed fabric, is laden with freshly harvested produce, all of it worked in individual ways to create a highly realistic effect. Each green bean, for example, is made and applied separately, while the potatoes nestling in the bottom are stitched and slightly gathered, and then stuffed from behind.

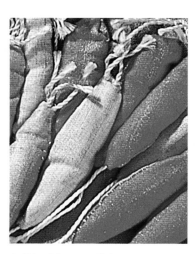

▲ **Eat your greens**
The dark green leafy vegetable is machine-embroidered in metallic thread to make separate leaves and veins.

▲ **Blushing radishes**
Radishes come in many shapes and colors. These are stuffed individually and have been given long white string roots and green cord leafy tops.

► **Root crops**
The new potatoes are almost hidden by the carrots, which have tops made separately from the stalks. The leaves are strips of fabric that have been slashed with the edges left raw.

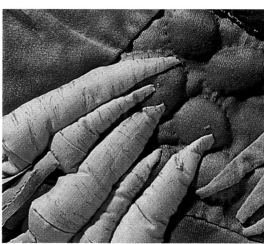

► **Berry berry nice**
The tiny gold dots on the strawberry fabric and the green thread tops create a very realistic crop of succulent-looking fruit.

◄ **Hidden daisy**
Almost hidden in the bottom left-hand corner is a delightful hand-embroidered daisy with applied leaves – a subtle and effective touch.

Seasonal Color

Depictions of plants are as varied on pictorial quilts as they are in real life, and once you have chosen a design format and a technique, selecting the colors is perhaps the next important decision. Although flowers come in almost every color of the rainbow, foliage is, usually, green. There are many shades of green, from the light, pale yellow of springtime leaves to the rich, deep shades of summer foliage. Then there are the yellow, orange, red, and russet hues that depict fall leaves in a way that is immediately recognizable.

" *I made a full-size, slightly simplified line drawing and traced the pattern pieces from it, adding seam allowances before I cut the fabric.* "

Gillian Clarke

▼ **August** Gillian Clarke
APPLIQUE, HAND QUILTING

A thresher raises his flail to separate the grain from the stalks in a scene based on a picture in a medieval prayerbook. The detail is finely wrought, from the lines of the plowed field and the quilted clouds in the hand-dyed sky to the serene face of the man himself.

▲ **Standing sheaf**
The grain, standing ready to thresh, is made from a subtly striped and quilted fabric, with the ripe tops in various colors lightly stuffed and applied individually.

The small flowers in the print ground fabric evoke the blooms of weeds left behind after the crop is cut.

Two small leaves cut from one of the fabrics have been applied, broderie-perse style, as they fall to the ground.

Close outline quilting has been worked sparingly to delineate and highlight various areas of the piece.

▲ **Mature-i-tree** Iris Taylor
MACHINE PIECING, HAND QUILTING

A very different technique has been used to create another fall impression here, with the effective use of squares and half-square triangles giving a strong sense of movement. The excellent choice of colors results from the maker's system of cutting shapes and arranging them on a board until she was satisfied.

> *Inspired by a blue tree displayed at a conference in Germany, I drafted this design and made spring, fall, and Christmas trees one day as a challenge.*

Iris Taylor

The machine quilting is stitched mainly in flower and leaf patterns.

Tiny red beads have been used to highlight the throat of each flower.

Garden Glory

Nowhere is the choice of color more important in pictorial quiltmaking than when the subjects are flowers and foliage. Green is the perceived color of leaves and stems, but can vary from almost yellow to almost blue, and some plants carry foliage that is red or gray or any of a number of other hues. Pictorial quiltmakers usually have copious scrap baskets, and searching for just the right shade and value to add contrast or depict a particular color for a flower is worth every effort.

◀ **Grass of Parnassus** Ingrid Taylor
PATCHWORK, MACHINE QUILTING

The bold white flowers are seen close up against an almost abstract background of muted flowerbed shades. The blocks are pieced in a kind of crazy-patchwork technique, with the foliage derived from the same method and design, but with the petal shapes in leafy colors instead of white.

▲ **Stalks and stems**
The stems of the flowers are worked in bright greens to make them stand out from the jumbled background of leaves and other flowers. An amazing number of leaf prints have been used to create the foliage.

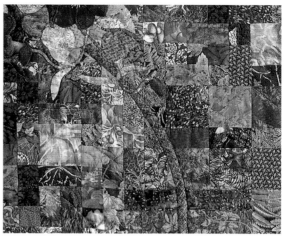

▼ Meet Me in the Garden
Dorothy M. Brinkman and Suzanne W. Brown
PATCHWORK, APPLIQUE, MACHINE QUILTING

Except for the brick wall, the background fabric is pieced from small squares in a watercolor technique of shading, with the beckoning open gate pieced into the design. The clematis vine with its twining bias-strip stems and varicolored leaves is appliquéd in a most realistic fashion.

▲ Secret support
From the top of the brick pillar, a metal pole fashioned from a wide bias strip arches over the gate to provide a support for the vine to climb. The mortar is made from light-colored straight strips sashed between each of the bricks and the rows.

The dark, heavy hinges add to the overall sense of realism displayed in this quilt.

The superb shading of the gate itself reinforces the quilt's three-dimensional quality.

The fan of quilting in the bottom right-hand corner adds realism to the bright colors of the fabrics used to depict the flowerbeds.

animals

ANIMALS OF ALL kinds can be found on quilts. Depicting the intricate makeup of most living creatures can be somewhat daunting for many quiltmakers, but the basic shapes of most animals – birds, fish, reptiles, mammals, and insects – can be simplified and distilled to a recognizable image for pictorial quilts.

Courageous Lion
Pieced and appliquéd by Christal Carter and machine quilted by Barbara Ford.

Simple Animal Shapes

Among the delights of creating a pictorial quilt is the fact that quite complicated images can be distilled into simple shapes that are relatively easy to work but give an unmistakable impression of the thing being represented. Children's picture books and coloring books are a good source of clean lines that can provide a starting point for a project.

▼ Cats (after Linda Bannock)
Elizabeth Platts
PATCHWORK, HAND QUILTING

Nine black-and-white cats have been constructed in horizontal rows, nearly all joined by the head to the legs of the one above. Only the background was quilted, making the cats stand out. They convey a feline haughtiness even without features on their simply-shaped faces and bodies.

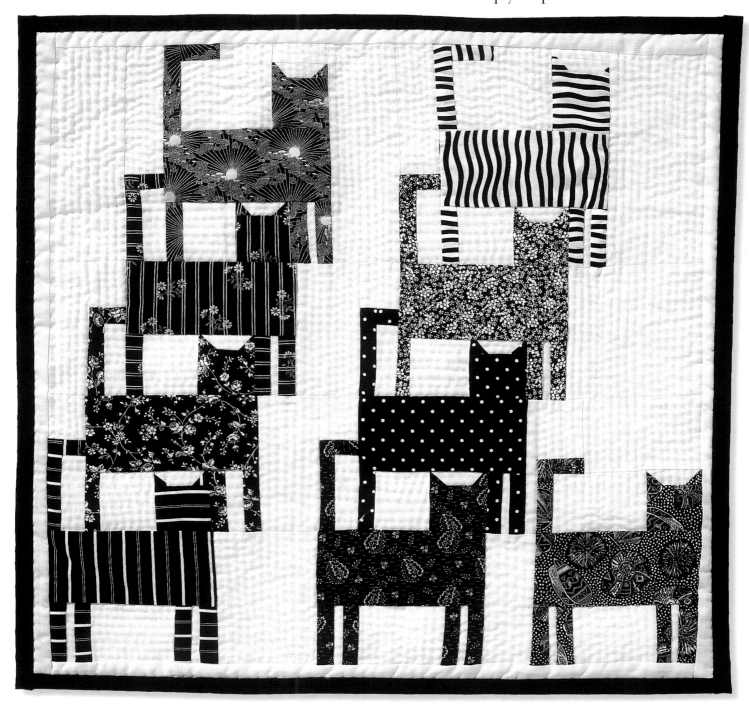

▲ **The Butterfly** Kate Spencer
STAINED-GLASS APPLIQUE, HAND QUILTING

This simple but effective shape, based on an embroidery
pattern and worked in stained-glass appliqué, began as a
workshop project. The maker traced the bold outlines directly
onto the background fabric and numbered each section on
the back before cutting out the pieces and applying them.

*The wings are fashioned from silk
sari fabric that has been stabilized
with a backing of a cotton and
polyester blend to give it body.*

A Colorful Menagerie

The natural living world provides endless scope for any designer, and makers of pictorial quilts are no exception. The results can be amusing, or shocking, or realistic, or somewhat abstract. Pets can be memorialized; wildlife that you may have encountered in exotic places can be immortalized.

Adapting source material can be tricky, but the secret most often lies in keeping the images simple and the lines clean. Embellishment – with quilting, embroidery, and beads and sequins, for example – is often a good way to give a lively look to a finished piece.

Reverse appliqué has been used with great effect to create the feathers.

Hand-embroidered eyelets represent the snowflakes falling on the great titmouse and the robin to the right. In certain circumstances, they could be used instead of tied quilting to hold the layers securely.

The quilting on the green background includes leaf shapes to enhance the woodpecker's nest high up in the tree trunk. The same device has been used on the toucan panel and with the parrots.

▶ **Cloudcuckooland** C. June Barnes
MACHINE APPLIQUE, MACHINE QUILTING

This highly appealing piece, showing recognizable but not quite realistic birdlife from around the world, is full of humor and interest. The brilliantly colored appliqué borders and sashing both delineate the individual images and bind the piece into a lively whole.

Cloudcuckooland *was inspired by a love of birds – they always seem to have such interesting expressions. The designs started as caricatures and ended up as more accurate studies as I progressed.*

C. June Barnes

Unlike the toucan's cherries, which are made from three different colors, the leaves on the parrots' bough are all the same fabric, but the satin-stitch outlining is worked in a light-colored thread on one side and a dark color on the other to provide a sense of shading.

▲ Gulls on the beach

Two gulls stand on a beautifully conceived shore staring out at a gray sea full of quilted waves and a cloudy sky. The pebbles at their feet go down to the sand, created from three strips of different fabric. The diagonal lines create a good sense of perspective in a limited space.

The different colors of thread along the satin-stitched shoreline create a feeling of waves breaking gently on the beach. The same technique has been used in the bottom right-hand panel to give a sense of movement and reflection on the surface of the lake.

Meander quilting creates an effective texture for several of the background areas and variously represents sand, snow, and ice, as well as the night sky behind the enchanting owl.

The outline around the freshly caught fish, satin-stitched in iridescent machine-embroidery thread, glistens like the water from which the crane has plucked it.

Birds of a Feather

Creating realistic representations, such as the feathers and beaks of birds, in fabric to make animals that look real needs careful planning. Sketch a design until you are happy with the arrangement of all the elements. Making a trial piece for each of the larger or more complicated components is also an excellent way of assessing where problems might occur and for figuring out various ways of approaching them.

▼ Where Land Meets Water
Inge Mardal and Steen Hougs
PIECING, APPLIQUE, MACHINE QUILTING

Depicting wading birds at the water's edge provides the quilters with several challenges: making the birds, differentiating between land and water, and creating realistic reflections. Careful choice of fabrics and color, and the variety of techniques used, have paid off handsomely.

The reeds on either side of the bank are reflected with great effect in the water.

The bird in the water and the one behind are shown as reflections in which the same fabric has been used with very different effect.

Subtle differences between the blues of the water combine with flowing shapes and curved quilting to create a feeling of water moving out to sea.

▼ Cape Gannets June Worman

PATCHWORK, APPLIQUE, MACHINE QUILTING

Wide strips of fabric have been used horizontally to make the background – sky, a sea pieced from blue and gray strips of random length, a beach, and a pool of brackish water – onto which the gannets in the flock have been applied individually. The birds are all variations of a few traced from an ornithology book and enlarged to different sizes.

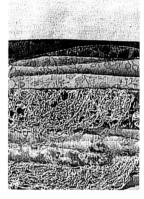

▲ Ocean waves
The foam of the breaking waves was made from machine embroidery worked in appropriate colors over dissolvable fabric and inserted in the seams of the pieced sea.

▲ A flock of gulls
The gannets at the water's edge, indicated by black and yellow dots of fabric paint and stitched beaks, meld into the larger foreground birds, which are also painted and embroidered.

Fish Tales

The rich variety of life found in the oceans of the world provides enormous scope for pictorial interpretation, and wonderful effects can be achieved by using unusual fabrics and embellishments. Embroidery by hand or machine, beads, buttons, shells, and found objects can be added to give texture.

The different forms of fish, together with the nonfishy creatures that inhabit the sea, can be simplified and rendered in so many countless ways that the first design decision to make is one of style – realism, abstraction, or comic. You will then find that other aspects – choice of fabric and background – will often follow.

▶ **Glory of the Deep** Hava Salter
APPLIQUE, HAND QUILTING, EMBROIDERY

The rich texture of this charming piece is both real and visual, with its design of a crowded sea and the wonderful variety of fabric weaves, prints, and colors. The carefully controlled quilting provides a superb feeling of constantly moving water.

The pieced background, made from a variety of printed and hand-dyed fabrics, gives a wonderful impression of the increasing depth of the ocean.

A felt starfish, embellished with rows of french knots, clings to the seabed rock.

▲ **Sucker for buttons**
A pink satin octopus displays its tentacles to reveal its suckers – rows of matching buttons.

▲ **Goldfish**
A goldfish, beautifully made from a rippling two-tone orange fabric, swims in its own current of rows of echo quilting.

A diaphanous jellyfish trails its string tentacles as it seeks its unsuspecting dinner among the school of silver fish nearby.

Several kinds of seaweed have been interpreted in appliqué and embroidery.

A lump of brain coral, a branch of coral concealing seahorses, and a group of small coral made from yo-yos, or Suffolk puffs, add to the variety of life forms.

> *I joined strips of different lengths and depth of color to make the background go from deep shades at the bottom to lighter at the top.*
>
> Hava Salter

Bold Effects

Among the most effective of all pictorial quilts are those that show clear but simple images worked in strong, carefully chosen colors. Many basic shapes are instantly identifiable – a cat, a butterfly, a house, a tiger, two lizards at play – and when they are worked in appropriate colors and given descriptive texture, a wonderfully bold quilt can result. Repeated shapes are also effective.

Keeping the main body of the piece simple can also give the quiltmaker leeway to add a complicated pieced border and plenty of embellishment.

> *I enjoy image-based work and like bold designs to give maximum impact and interest.*
>
> Helen Keenan

▶ You Go First, I'll Follow
Helen Keenan
APPLIQUE, REVERSE APPLIQUE, MACHINE QUILTING

The quiltmaker decided to use appliqué and random piecing to memorialize two lizards whose antics kept her and her family entertained during a hot summer vacation. The fiery background and hot, dusty colors in the border evoke a strong sense of place.

▲ **Star flower**
The star flowers and the lizards themselves have been reverse appliquéd by hand, while the background meander quilting and the outlining are machine stitched.

▶ **Border differences**
The side borders are made of Log Cabin blocks and the top and bottom from braid-effect squares. All are pieced from random-sized strips and heavily quilted.

◀ **Square dance**
Each corner is made from a different fabric chosen to go with the color of the star flower, while all the quilting in the border is stitched using a brassy gold metallic thread.

Zebra and Tiger

Recreating mammals in a realistic form presents a particular challenge to the pictorial quiltmaker. It can be useful to have some basic drawing skills, but is certainly not essential. Books about animals often have excellent photographs or drawings that can be adapted (see page 20). Tracings can be altered and enlarged, or perhaps someone you know can create the image you are after. Or you can depend on the shape and a few salient features of the animal – a zebra's stripes, a horse's mane, a monkey's tail – to convey the idea. Colors can be portrayed realistically, or they can move into the realm of fantasy without forsaking the recognizable image.

▼ The Quilter's Ark
Susan Peakin
REVERSE APPLIQUE, MACHINE QUILTING

The maker of this quilt works in highly textured layers. In this pictorial departure from her more usual abstract images, she began with the hand-dyed landscape. Then she added the other fabrics – for the hand-dyed giraffe and the print for the zebra's stripes – before laying the black fabric, which appears on the zebra's body and the giraffe's feet, on top.

Wavy lines of machine quilting, worked after all the cutting was done, give an impression of shimmering heat.

All the lines were marked and stitched with zigzag over a gimp cord before being cut away carefully layer by layer.

▲ Zebra's head
The features – eyes, nose, and muzzle – are all suggested simply, but to great effect, by clever shaping and placement.

A narrow binding of tiger-striped fabric provides the perfect edging. It has also been used to cover the seams on the back of the quilt that result from the piecing process.

A tiny broderie-perse dragonfly – the smallest of the tiger's eleven friends – hovers above the watering hole.

▲ Tiger, Tiger ... and His Eleven Friends Jenni Dobson
"FRACTURED" PIECING, APPLIQUE, MACHINE QUILTING

A playful-looking tiger is caught in a shaft of light by the water's edge in a dense jungle landscape. The superb choice of fabrics is highlighted by the abrupt but effective changes of shading as the sunlight filters through the variety of different leaves. The bright-colored butterflies are among the eleven animal friends of the title that enliven the quilt.

▶ **Crouching cub**
The tiger cub, with its realistic-looking face, was made using a technique, devised by well-known quilter Linda Straw, of working from the back. Straight embroidery stitches indicate its whiskers and outline its ears.

“ *This hanging was the eleventh piece I have made for a wonderful client, who gave it to a grandchild.* ”

Jenni Dobson

Natural Representations

Sometimes the images contained in quilts are best described as representational. They are pictures of recognizable forms, often stylized and juxtaposed in such a way that they move in the direction of abstraction. Animal and plant shapes are particularly adaptable for this type of pictorial quiltmaking because the variety found in nature means that things can be given a form realistic enough to be appreciated by the viewer, but one that also creates an overall pattern such as can be found in traditional geometric quilt designs.

▼ There's No Place Like Home
Marta Amundson
REVERSE APPLIQUE, MACHINE QUILTING

The strong contrasts of color and design give this elegantly conceived and executed quilt an overall abstract pattern that needs closer examination. Only then does the viewer see that each quadrant consists of reversed images of an Australian animal – crocodile, platypus, kangaroo, and woodpecker.

Heavy meander or stipple quilting is used to knock back the white areas, both in the background and the images.

The antipodean theme is reinforced by the playful koala bears quilted in the red borders.

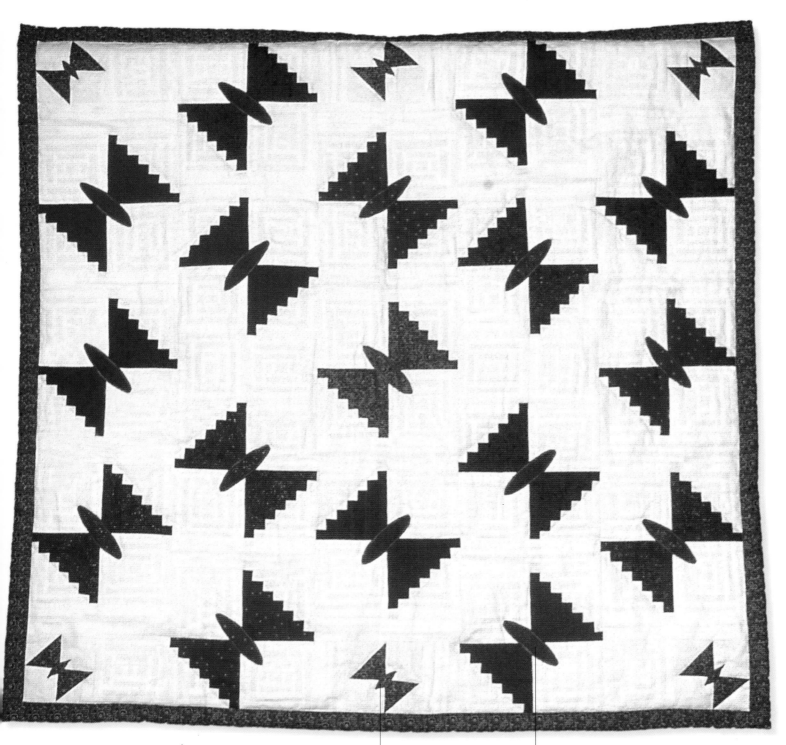

▲ **Life Is a Butterfly** Anne Hardcastle
PATCHWORK, MACHINE APPLIQUE

Stylized butterflies made from a variety of red fabrics dance across this beautifully designed and worked quilt. The technique used for the piecing is Log Cabin patchwork, with the setting carefully planned to give a random look to the placement and spacing of each image.

The small butterflies at each corner and in the center top and bottom are small pieced Hourglass blocks.

The realism of the images is provided in great measure by the body machine appliquéd between the wings of each butterfly.

figures

PORTRAITS and figures have long been a part of artistic tradition, but using fabric as the medium for creating human likenesses is a recent development. This section illustrates a variety of ways in which contemporary textile artists and quilters have interpreted the human form.

Solomon and the Shulammite
Diana Brockway

Viewing Figures

Because movies and their images are so universal a part of modern culture, the Hollywood movie in particular offers a huge selection of ideas. You could recreate a favorite scene or a classic movie poster of the past, or combine elements from your favorite movies into one quilt.

Movie characters are often associated with particular costumes or props, which you can use as part of your composition to help to identify them. Bringing so many immediately identifiable motifs into one coherent work needs careful planning and organization. Remember to balance shapes and color values (see page 26) for a composition with maximum impact.

▶ **And the Nominations Are …**
Claire Scott
APPLIQUE, EMBROIDERY, MACHINE QUILTING

This charming and intricate quilt is filled with icons of the cinema from Oscar himself to a pile of discarded ticket stubs in the corner. Each segment of the film roll contains a character or device that will be recognizable to movie fans the world over.

> *This is a quilt for my daughter, a fan of the cinema. She drew the working designs from which I made templates.*
>
> Claire Scott

▲ **Marilyn**
Monroe's famous billowing skirt is made of chiffon gathered and ruched to stand realistically away from her shapely legs.

◀ **Oscar**
One of the best-known statuettes in the world, the golden Academy Award emblem has been worked in gold lamé.

▲ **Darth and Dorothy**
The flowing capes of the "Star Wars" warriors are simple and unembellished, while Dorothy and her friends on the road to Oz, are decorated with embroidery.

▶ **The Full Monty**
Backs can be almost as expressive as the front of figures, as the attentiveness of the audience watching the end of the act from "backstage" shows.

Heeere's Groucho!

Creating an instantly recognizable likeness of a famous figure, or even a member of your own family, presents difficulties. But picking out traits that are associated with a well-known image – Groucho's eyebrows and cigar, for example – can provide a good starting point. Make these props or personal characteristics a central part of your design.

Drawing the piece full-size on either plain or freezer paper (see pages 44 and 45) means that you can see the effect of the overall design and make changes before cutting into the fabric. The drawing itself can then be cut up to make templates for each design element.

▶ **Groucho** Margaret Standish
APPLIQUE, MACHINE EMBROIDERY, MACHINE QUILTING

Perspective has its place in pictures other than landscapes, as this delightful quilt illustrates wonderfully. The main focus – the silver screen – has been offset to lead the eye deep into the space, and lines of meander quilting from the side edges into the screen are positioned to draw the eye toward this crucial element.

The graduated sizes of the receding rows of seats from the back to the front of the house and the spacing between rows on the central carpet enhance the three-dimensional feeling.

▶ **Rays of light**
The light bouncing off the screen onto the walls of the cinema is made from hundreds of tiny pieces of fabric ranging from pale gray to black. They are bonded to the background fabric and machine quilted with variegated metallic machine-embroidery thread.

Careful choice of fabrics makes the difference between a quilt that "works" and one than does not. Black felt has been used for Groucho's hair, mustache, and the famous bushy eyebrows.

Margaret Standish cut into a good black skirt to make Groucho's suit jacket because, she says, "it was just the right material" – true devotion to her art.

Each head in the audience has its own hairstyle, and therefore its own personality, even when seen from the back. The use of three-dimensional touches like the feather in the pink hat and Groucho's pink satin carnation add to the overall effect.

The back row of the cinema is a traditional place for courtship. The relationship of the couple on the right seems to have progressed further than that of Rambo and his two ladies on the opposite side of the aisle.

Face the Future

Faces are notoriously difficult to work in fabric. The shading depends on the colors chosen to convey light and shadow, and the irregularity of human features means that realistic lines and contours can only be constructed if small, often strangely shaped pieces are combined, making it hard to work close-up views that look natural.

These three – one full front, one half-turned, the third in profile – are moving to face the rosy dawn of a new millennium rising behind them. Liz Hands' unique technique allows her to create remarkably evocative versions of the human face.

▶ **Face the Future – Millennium Dawn** Liz Hands
ENGLISH PIECING, FOUNDATION PIECING, MACHINE QUILTING, MACHINE EMBROIDERY

The maker creates curves that follow the contours of a face by tracing a distorted grid over her original drawing. She then enlarges the tracing to use as a full-size pattern and works the patchwork by a combination of foundation piecing – stitching directly onto paper or fabric backing – and the English paper-piecing method.

◀ **Looking ahead**
All the features, but especially the eyes, are the elements that give a natural finish to a fabric rendering of a face. The careful shaping and precise positioning of the white highlights in each case contributes greatly to the realistic look of the women.

The machine-embroidered clocks and
numerals have been worked by shading
the edges with darker thread.

Each of the figures is "wearing" a
piece of the wheel-patterned fabric
used to make the border, a device that
gives cohesion to the overall design.

Careful shading and satin-
stitching of the strands
make it easy to see which
hair belongs to which face.

Backgrounds can be
strip-pieced and cut,
then stepped like a
bargello pattern.

Symbolic Figures

The portrayal of realism is difficult in any medium, and quilters, like painters and sculptors, use symbolism to depict things in a way that is immediately recognizable. However, the approach is not necessarily the same, even if the influences, locations, or source material are similar, and several different quiltmaking techniques may be used to achieve the desired end. Some quiltmakers paint parts of their designs directly on the cloth for freehand expression.

Flocks of a humorous species of bird march across the top and bottom of the quilt.

Another symbol of Africa, the elephant, watches somewhat warily from the border.

▼ **Protective shield**
The shields are all made from the same fabrics and reversed to add a sense of vitality to the overall composition. The plain areas are more heavily quilted than the patterned ones.

▲ **Zulu** C. June Barnes
APPLIQUE, HAND QUILTING

In the maker's native Africa, the Zulu tribe was famed for the height and prowess of its warriors. Here she evokes memories of her childhood through the use of earth colors and tribal symbols that would have been familiar and understood in her African-born European community as well.

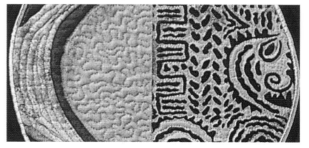

▼ Sahel Hollis Chatelain
HAND PAINTING, MACHINE QUILTING

This evocative piece is a wholecloth quilt (made from a single piece of cloth), a large-scale drawing that combines three photographs taken on a trip among the Fulani people of West Africa. The women of the tribe are considered the most beautiful in the region, located south of the Sahara Desert, and the quilt is the maker's tribute to the beauty she "discovered in this part of the world."

The piece was painted with thickened fiber-active dyes, then washed and machine quilted.

▲ The baobab tree
The baobab is known in the barren areas where it grows as the tree of life, since it provides food and medicine, as well as shade from the fierce equatorial sun. By painting it, the quiltmaker has achieved a realism that would have been difficult to create by piecing fabrics.

When the maker spent a week on a drawing trip in a village in northern Benin, the young girl pictured on the left of the tree became her constant companion.

Abstract Realism

The mixing of abstract images with realistic ones is very much a part of contemporary art and design, and pictorial quiltmakers can use the juxtaposition to great advantage. Paring a form down to its basic lines with little detail means it can be recognizable as, say, a human figure, which can then be combined with other bold abstract shapes to make an exciting piece of work.

Inspiration can be found in many places. The paintings and sculptures of many Post-Impressionist artists can provide a wealth of ideas. Tribal art and imagery is full of often bold and stylized forms that adapt very well to being reproduced in fabric.

▶ **Mask** C. June Barnes
APPLIQUE, HAND QUILTING

Strong colors, bold diagonal lines, simple shapes, and superb workmanship all contribute to the effectiveness of this lively wall hanging. The appliqué technique, devised by Linda Straw, is worked from the back, and each color is outlined in satin stitch using thread that matches each bright solid fabric. The two-tone border adds another diagonal to the overall design.

66 *I was born in Northern Rhodesia, now Zambia, and I suppose the tribal influences are in my blood.* 99

C. June Barnes

The uneven shapes and the lightning zigzags enhance the traditional tribal feeling of the mask.

The colors chosen for the various pieces match those in the brightly colored border fabric, which has also been used for the binding.

Matisse loved forms from nature, particularly birds, flowers, and leaves, all of which have been used here.

The figures, with their uplifted arms, express a joyfulness that brings pleasure to the viewer, reinforced by the bright saturated colors that Matisse also used in his work.

Straight parallel lines of machine quilting worked in a metallic holographic thread, add texture and overall consistency.

> *Using a collection of Matisse postcards, I chose images that interested me and experimented with free-cut shapes using colored paper and scissors, just as Matisse had done.*
>
> **Pippa Abrahams**

▲ Mad about Matisse Pippa Abrahams
PIECING, APPLIQUE, MACHINE QUILTING

The inspiration for this exuberant pictorial quilt was French artist Henri Matisse. A semi-invalid for part of his life, he was deprived of his beloved paints, and to keep his creativity alive, he began to work from his bed with paper cutouts in bright colors and bold shapes. Because the images are simple, they adapt well to appliqué techniques. The quilt represents a complete departure for the maker, who more often works with geometric forms and experienced "an exhilarating sense of freedom" in abandoning geometry's constraints.

places

PICTORIAL QUILTS are often conceived and executed to commemorate or celebrate a certain place – a vacation idyll, a birthplace, a home-town, a secret hideaway, perhaps. To distill the essence of a location and interpret it in fabric presents quiltmakers with opportunities that many cannot resist.

Venetian Adventure (detail)
Jackie Evans. Quilted by Betty Standiferd.

Architectural Masterpieces

B uildings have strong geometric components that can be simplified and stylized more easily than, for instance, people. Older buildings with particular architectural features, such as arches or columns, offer many different shapes, as do windows, which can be rendered with embellishments or decorative stitching. Some quiltmakers prefer to take their inspiration from a photograph or drawing to recreate a house or other building, while others take elements of several different places and combine them into a coherent whole that, despite being a fantasy, gives an unmistakable impression of a particular location.

▼ **Old Amsterdam** Ans Peschar
APPLIQUE, EMBROIDERY, HAND QUILTING

A picture-postcard view of a row of houses across a canal in the old city has been interpreted to give a feeling of the city of today, with its cars and bicycles. The same blue patterned material has been used for both the water and the sky, and the choice of fabrics for the street and the houses is superb.

The border is pieced, mainly from the fabrics used in the work, and bound in blue.

Ribbon and strips of felt have been used to create architectural details.

The embroidered details, such as the curtains, add charm and richness of texture.

▼ Millennium – Midnight in Moscow Jennie Lewis
APPLIQUE, HAND QUILTING

The onion domes associated with the Russian Orthodox Church, colorful against a starry sky of midnight blue, place this quilt, made to commemorate the beginning of a new millennium, in the center of Moscow.

▲ Golden domes
Curved lines of machine satin stitch enhance the rounded outline of the dome, while the decorative gold-metallic stitching just underneath gives a 3D effect.

Tiny multicolored stars have been imprinted on the background.

A variety of decorative machine stitches have been used to work and embellish the appliqué.

The diagonal lines of machine quilting have been stitched using metallic thread, adding to the twinkling effect of a star-filled sky.

Traveler's Tales

The idea of commemorating a journey or a special trip appeals to many quiltmakers, and a scenic or pictorial piece can bring back pleasant memories years later. The travel theme can be one simple image adapted from a postcard or snapshot, or it can be elaborate and include more than one aspect of your travels.

Methods of transportation provide another area that can be used effectively in a quilt. A favorite car or boat, ships at sea, trains, and aircraft, with their clean lines and familiar connotations, all provide interesting subjects.

> *I have long admired the poster-like quality of 1930s artwork with its bold use of color and simple lines which translate into fabric so well.*
>
> Jane E. Petty

▲ Place-name borders
City names – each with a local landmark or concept, such as the Manhattan cocktail in "New York" – make a lively border.

▶ Going Places Jane E. Petty
APPLIQUE, HAND QUILTING

This fabric travel poster evokes the excitement and luxury of foreign travel during the 1930s. It illustrates all the methods that were used most often at the time, from the steam train on its viaduct to the ocean liner sailing from the city skyline toward the glamorous faraway pier. The maker has incorporated an amazing number of nostalgic images into the piece, designed to bring out the vagabond in us all.

◀ Skyline
The instantly recognizable shapes of the Empire State and Chrysler buildings dominate the dense, sunlit island of Manhattan. The buildings and the patches of background are outline quilted.

◀ Passenger and train
A lone passenger watches the steam engine emerging from the tunnel, its smoke billowing out in multitoned layers of gray and white.

▲ Touring car
The green roadster with its 1930s shape and European license plate projects an image of comfort and style as it cruises over the brow of a hill on a quiet country lane.

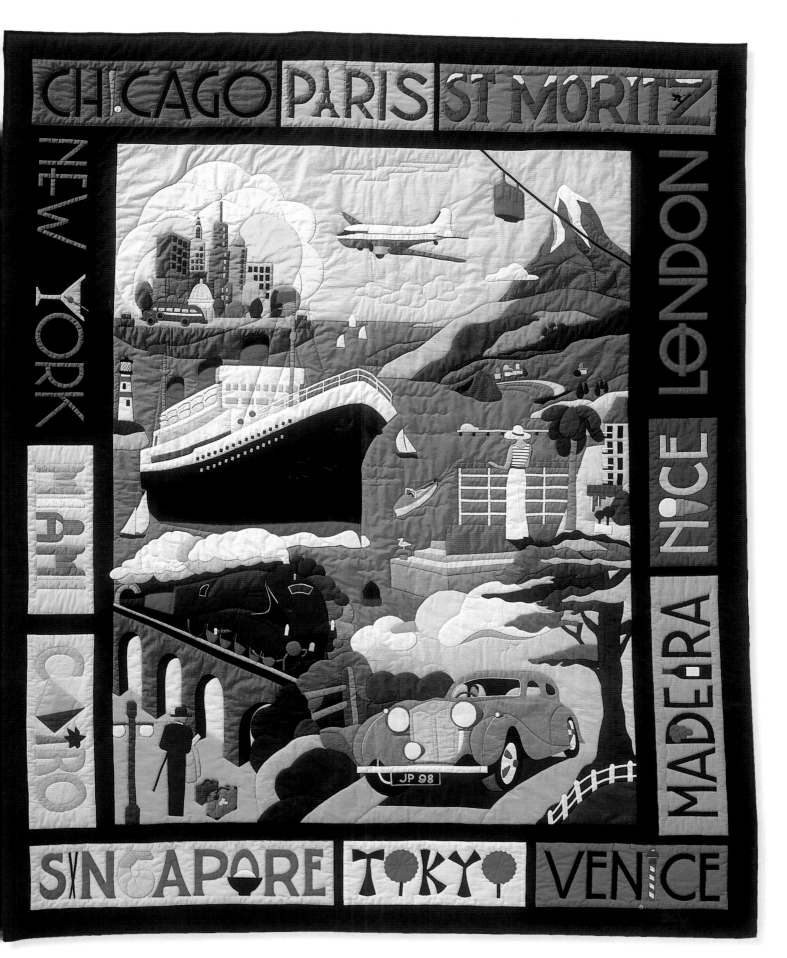

A Celebration of Home

Many pictorial quilts commemorate a place or an event, much as the Baltimore album quilts did. These memorials are frequently made as group projects, perhaps to celebrate an anniversary or raise money for a local project. A number of ambitious efforts were constructed around the celebration of the millennium in the year 2000 and will stand as permanent records of the history of a particular area. A smaller group of such projects have been made by individuals, and will no doubt become tributes to the skill of the makers as well.

▶ Cissa Ceastre – Chichester
Patricia McLaughlin
PIECED BACKGROUND, APPLIQUE, MACHINE QUILTING

This commemoration of the English cathedral city of Chichester is the product of extensive research by its maker. After she confirmed the accuracy of her information and obtained permission where necessary, she made detailed working drawings for each element and only then decided on the overall layout of the piece.

▶ The cathedral
The cathedral, built in 1075, dominates the scene, set against a hand-dyed landscape background of the South Downs. It is framed by a Norman arch, a device incorporated to recognize and honor the building's Norman origins.

▶ Saint Richard
The patron saint of the city of Chichester, whose resting place is a focus for modern pilgrims, stands resplendent in his bishop's robes. The embellishment on his clothing, miter, bible, and the top of his staff have all been machine quilted in metallic thread.

▶ Celtic warriors
Two fearsome Celtic warriors in tartan battle dress look down on the history that followed them. Each piece of appliqué was worked by hand on a lightweight backing "slip" and applied by the turned edge technique.

◀ Bishop gardens
The colorful garden has been given texture and realism with free machine quilting. The maker used the needle "in the same way as a pencil" to create leaves, vines, and tufts of grass, as well as a drystone wall, a thatched roof, a brick boundary, and the pink path.

Firework Celebration

One of the trends in recent years at quilt fairs, festivals, and exhibitions has been the setting of special competitions with an overall theme, many of which lend themselves to pictorial interpretation. The quilts shown here were both worked for a Millennium challenge at the British National Patchwork Association's annual exhibition in London and use the idea of fireworks on New Year's Eve 1999/2000 to great, and very different, effect.

Working within the guidelines of a challenge theme can be an inspiration to broaden horizons. The wide variety of fabrics and colors chosen will inevitably lead to a broad range of interpretation. When the choice of technique is also left to the quilter, who knows what might result?

▼ New Days – Old City
Diane Baker and Chris Hughes
PATCHWORK, MACHINE EMBROIDERY, HAND QUILTING

Traditional Log Cabin blocks are used to create buildings and background, with shiny fabric in the central windows to give a sense of light and life. The fireworks, machine embroidered in metallic threads, streak across the night sky, and the clocks in the border reinforce the idea of a new era in an old city.

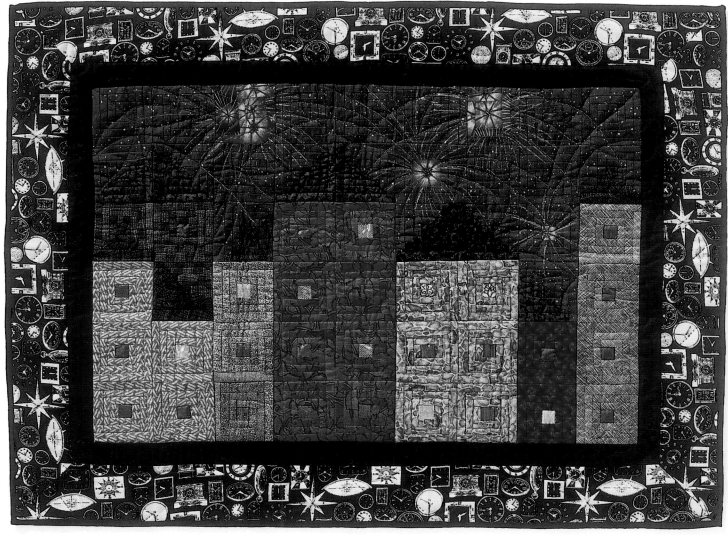

▲ **London 2000** Teresa Dunn
PATCHWORK, APPLIQUE, MACHINE QUILTING

The background, showing a montage of London's monuments, was strip pieced, with London's skyline dominated by Big Ben. The sky was machine quilted in a curved pattern, and both Big Ben and the river Thames were outlined in gold.

◀ **Fireworks**
The impressive showers of the exploding fireworks were cut freehand and machine stitched in gold thread to represent the trails of light.

Interior Places

Many places that can be recreated in a pictorial quilt are indoors, not out. A favorite room, a quiet corner, a cabinet or shelf of curios or books can all provide source material for interesting, highly personal work. Dishes on a kitchen counter or a table set for a festive meal can be wittily portrayed in fabric. The viewer of a scene inside a house or other building can be positioned to look out of a door or window into the exterior vista beyond. Or, the door can be firmly shut or the curtains drawn to enclose the area.

▶ **Ex Libris** Melyn Robinson
PATCHWORK, MACHINE QUILTING

A collection of titles from the classics of literature stand in no particular order in a bookcase pieced using an irregular Log Cabin block. The way in which some shelves are crammed with upright spines, while on others books lean across to fill gaps, adds to the realistic nature of this piece.

▼ **Bonnard's Window II** Margaret Ramsay
PATCHWORK, MACHINE QUILTING

Pierre Bonnard was a French Impressionist painter whose viewpoint is summed up in this quilt. The viewer is indoors in the shadows looking through the open door to a glorious day outside. The choice of colors highlights the realism and the mood, from the glow of the wooden table to the dark wall behind the door.

The book titles were printed from a computer using different typefaces and sizes onto hand-dyed fabric, which was then cut into strips of varying widths and lengths.

Rows of machine quilted spirals cover the piece from top to bottom with the effect of brushstrokes.

Index

Acknowledgments and Sources

Author's Acknowledgments
To David.
With much appreciation to Juliet Webster and the Patchwork Association, Quilt Events, Creative Exhibitions Limited, and the Quilters Guild of the British Isles, for all their help in contacting the quiltmakers, and heartfelt thanks to all the quiltmakers who allowed us to feature their work. Happy quilting to them all.

Further Quilting Information
If you have enjoyed this book and would like to see more examples of pictorial quilts by leading contemporary quiltmakers, visit one of the shows organized by quilter's associations, such as the Patchwork Association in the United Kingdom and the American Quilter's Society in the United States.

There are numerous helpful resources available, including quilting books, museums, clubs, classes, magazines, and mail-order catalogues. The Internet can provide wide exposure to most of them, and the following abbreviated source list will get you started:

Free Stuff for Quilters on the Internet. Judy Heim & Gloria Hansen. Concord, CA: C&T Publishing, Inc. (1998)

United Kingdom:
The Patchwork Association
c/o Traplet Publications Ltd
Traplet House
Severn Drive
Upton-upon-Severn
Worcestershire WR8 0JL
Tel: (01684) 594505
www.traplet.co.uk

The Quilter's Guild of the British Isles
Room 190
Dean Clough
Halifax HX3 5AX
Tel: (01422) 347669
the.quilter@easynet.co.uk

United States:
American Quilter's Society
P.O. Box 3290
Paducah, KY 42002
Tel: (270) 898-7903
www.AQSquilt.com/workarea/lasso

The National Quilting Association
P.O. Box 393
Ellicott City, MD 21041
Tel: (410) 461-5733
www.his.com/-queenb/nqa/

The New England Quilt Museum
18 Shattuck Street
Lowell, MA 01852
Tel: (978) 452-4207
www.nequiltmuseum.org

Studio Art Quilt Associates
P.O. Box 287
Dexter, OR 97431
Tel: (541) 937-8061
www.saqa.com

World Wide Quilting Page
www.ttsw.com/MainQuiltingPage.html